The Music of
AARON COPLAND

D1407449

THE MUSIC OF

Aaron Copland

Neil Butterworth

With a Preface by
André Previn

**TOCCATA
PRESS**

First published in 1985 by Toccata Press
© Neil Butterworth, 1985
Appendix 1 © CBS

Music examples drawn by the author.

British Library Cataloguing in Publication Data

Butterworth, Neil
 The music of Aaron Copland.
 1. Copland, Aaron
 I. Title
 780'.92'4   ML410.C7

 ISBN 0-907689-07-8 (cased)
 ISBN 0-907689-08-6 (paper)

Set in 11 on 12 point Baskerville
 by Alan Sutton Publishing, Gloucester.
Printed by Nene Litho, and bound by Woolnough Binding,
 Wellingborough.

Contents

Preface by
ANDRÉ PREVIN

Aaron Copland is such a towering figure in twentieth-century music that he has become synonymous with American music. Time and time again, when my colleagues and I are asked for the inclusion of an American work in a concert (particularly in Europe), what the presenters are actually requesting is a work of Copland's. This kind of total identification with nationalism in music has also lapsed into the somewhat dangerous field of commercially cynical imitations; for example, endless film scores attempting to depict certain 'outdoor' aspects of America – to be specific, the West and New England – steal blithely from those pages of Copland's most famous scores which can be imitated but never actually duplicated. What is obvious to musicians is that these desperate echoes serve only to illuminate how wonderful the original creations are. It is not unlike the attitude that 'British' should always sound like Elgar. (How many fraudulent versions of 'Land of Hope and Glory' have you heard?)

A fascinating aspect of Copland's compositions is that his particular voice, his handwriting, is discernable even in his most dissonant works. It is undeniable that *Connotations* and *Inscape* are forays into serialism, but within their austere and rather forbidding structures his personal use of the sound of the orchestra, the voicings of the chords and the intervallic leaps in the melodic lines are unmistakable and could not possibly have been written by anyone else. I once heard a recording of a piece for mandolin by Beethoven, and although the jangling seemed to make the composer's name an improbability, truly giant creators have been above the pragmatic advantages of being chameleons; and Copland belongs to that handful of twentieth-century composers who have managed to be instantly identifiable.

His enormous influence has not been limited to the score page. His many books are read and studied assiduously, and no one has written on musical matters with more lucidity and strength. All his life long he has been a promoter and a staunch advocate of new music, and many are the composers whose work has been heard because of one of Copland's recommendations. His advice to students never comes from the ivory tower of fame but takes the form of friendly conversation between colleagues, and the young people fortunate enough to have crossed his path in Tanglewood (the summer school run by the Boston Symphony) have been enriched immeasurably. He is a fine conductor and no one does his works with more élan or rhythmic insistence.

Having been born in 1900, he would now certainly be eligible to take on the role of a reclusive grand old man. But he is not suited for the part. He is just as curious as ever in examining the new and experimental, he goes right on conducting, and the thought of a future work by him is as eagerly awaited as it has been for the past fifty years. He is a great man, and no one connected with music can be anything but grateful for his presence.

Introduction

For musicians throughout the world, Aaron Copland represents all that characterises the United States. In his music
he reflects the activity of urban life on the one hand and the
vastness of open spaces on the other. His occasional use of
folk songs with modal harmony, the melodic and rhythmic
elements of jazz and popular music, the aggressive
dissonance of a machine age are all the natural expressions
of a lad from Brooklyn who has absorbed the life and music
around him.

In a BBC radio broadcast to mark his 80th birthday,[1]
Copland said:

> I was trying to write music in the serious field which would
> be as American in quality as the jazz boys had been able to
> manage in the light field.

Yet his background was not that of the original settlers.
His parents, Lithuanian Jews, arrived separately in America
towards the close of the 19th century as part of the large
exodus of refugees fleeing religious and ethnic persecution
at home.

In his early twenties, when he first attended the classes of
Nadia Boulanger in Paris, he epitomised for his fellow
students all that was typically American. At that time on the
international music scene, George Gershwin's fame had
spread to Europe, and the popular music which swept
through France and England was principally imported from
New York. After his return to America at the end of the
decade, Copland rejected the overtly jazzy style he had
briefly adopted, and after a period of ascetic astringency,
produced scores of a decidedly American flavour, at first
associated mainly with ballet.

During that 80th birthday broadcast, he jokingly
remarked:

[1] Radio 3, 12 November 1980.

Copland, photographed by Malcolm Crowthers in 1981 in the late November sun, outside his home in Peekskill, New York.

The attraction of folk song was that it was an easy way to sound American. They're free – anyone can use them.

Although not his most critically admired works, the three 'folk' ballets, *Billy the Kid*, *Rodeo* and *Appalachian Spring* represent the authentic Copland sound and are likely to remain the music by which he will best be remembered to generations to come. Through them he has proved to the musical public at large that a serious American composer exists who can be set beside the masters of Europe.

My own study of Copland's music began in 1962 with a thesis on his symphonic works. On its completion nearly three years later, he said to me, 'You must know me better than I know myself!' That is a claim I do not accept; but my own researches thereafter did lead me to explore the whole of his output – which has resulted in this book.

I have concentrated upon Copland the composer; Copland the man is being revealed through his memoirs, the first volume[2] of which, prepared with the assistance of Vivien Perlis, appeared in November 1984. My intention has been to provide an introduction to his music to whet the appetite – which I hope will add to an increased interest in his works.

[2] *Copland*, Vol. 1: 1900–1942, Faber & Faber, London and Boston.

Acknowledgements

It is of constant surprise to me that no further studies of Copland's music have appeared since the two pioneering books by Arthur Berger in 1953 and Julia Smith in 1955. I am indebted to both for providing the initial impetus and a wealth of factual information that launched me on my musical journey.

I am most grateful to Mr Copland for reading the manuscript at various stages and offering corrections and additional material. I should also like to thank my daughter Clare and Mrs Carol Crawford who between them typed the indecipherable manuscript, and Martin Anderson, whose helpful advice on content and presentation kept me pointed in the right direction. David Brown, Michael George and Guy Rickards helped with the proof-reading. Virgil Thomson deserves my thanks both for supplying, very promptly, the photograph by Thérèse Bonney on p. 36 and for allowing me to quote extensively from his writings. Phillip Ramey provided advice, practical help and photographs with promptness, good humour and enthusiasm. And Milein Cosman's characteristic warmth was confirmed once more by the readiness with which she agreed to the reproduction of her drawings, published here in Appendix 1. The handwriting which graces the cover and chapter-headings of this book belongs to Caroline Hobbs, whose sharp eye also provided useful comments on the text.

For permission to reprint copyright material, I am grateful to the following publishers: Barrie and Jenkins and Hutchinson Publishing Group (Wilfrid Mellers, *Music in a New Found Land*); J.M. Dent and Sons (Arnold Whittall, *Music since the First World War*); André Deutsch and Doubleday and Co. (Aaron Copland, *On Music*); Dennis Dobson and Alfred A. Knopf (Harold Clurman, *The Fervent Years* and Darius Milhaud, *Notes without Music*, translated by Donald Evans, edited by Rollo H. Myers); E.P. Dutton and Co. (Julia Smith, *Aaron Copland*); Harvard University Press (Aaron Copland, *Music and Imagination*); McGraw-Hill Book Co. and Macdonald and Co. (Aaron Copland, *The New Music 1900–1960* and *What to Listen for in Music*); W.W. Norton and Co. and Princeton University Press (Benjamin Boretz and Edward T. Cone, *Perspectives on American Composers* and Joseph Machlis, *Introduction to Contemporary Music*); and Oxford University Press (Arthur Berger, *Aaron Copland*). Extracts from the following works of Aaron Copland are reproduced by kind permission of Mr Copland, who is the copyright holder, and of Boosey & Hawkes Music

Publishers Ltd., the sole licensees and publishers (the date after each work is the year of copyright): *Appalachian Spring* (1945), *Billy the Kid* (1941 and 1978), *Canticle of Freedom* (1955 and 1968), Clarinet Concerto (1949), *Connotations* (1953), *Dance Panels* (1965), *Dance Symphony* (Arrow Music Press, 1931; assigned to Aaron Copland), *Danzón Cubano* (1943 and 1949), Duo (1971), *Emblems* (1965), First Symphony (Arrow Music Press, 1931; assigned to Aaron Copland), *Four Piano Blues* (1949), *Inscape* (1968), *In the Beginning* (1947), *Lincoln Portrait* (1943), *Music for a Great City* (1965), *Music for the Theatre* (Arrow Music Press, 1932; assigned to Aaron Copland), Nonet (1962), Piano Concerto (Arrow Music Press, 1929; assigned to Aaron Copland); *Piano Fantasy* (1957), Piano Quartet (1951), Piano Sonata (1942), *Piano Variations* (Arrow Music Press, 1932; assigned to Aaron Copland), *Prairie Journal* (1940), *Preamble for a Solemn Occasion* (1953), *The Red Pony* (1951), *Rodeo* (1962), *Rondino* (Arrow Music Press, 1940; assigned to Aaron Copland), *El Salón México* (1959), *The Second Hurricane* (C.C. Birchard, 1938, 1939; assigned to Aaron Copland), *Short Symphony* (1955), *Statements* (1947), *Symphonic Ode* (1957), *The Tender Land* (1956), Third Symphony (1947), *Three Latin-American Sketches* (*Danza de Jalisco*, 1968; *Estribillo* and *Paisaje Mexicano*, 1975; *Danza de Jalisco*, orchestral arrangement, 1975), *Threnody I* (1972), *Threnody II* (1977), *Twelve Poems of Emily Dickinson* (1951), *Ukulele Serenade* (B. Schott's Söhne, 1928; assigned to Aaron Copland), Violin Sonata (1944), *Vitebsk* (Arrow Music Press, 1934; assigned to Aaron Copland), *Vocalise* (Alphonse Leduc, 1929; assigned to Aaron Copland).

N.B.

List of Illustrations

I. Early Years — New York and Paris
(1900–1924)

Aaron Copland was born in Brooklyn on 14 November 1900, the youngest of five children of Harris and Sarah Kaplan. Harris Kaplan was born in Shavel, near Kovno, in Lithuania in 1860. At the age of fifteen, he decided to emigrate to America to avoid the increasing persecution of Jews in Russia and to escape compulsory military service. When, on his entry to England, an immigration officer mistakenly wrote his name as Harris Copland, he decided to retain this spelling. For nearly two years he lived in London, Glasgow and Manchester. He arrived in Brooklyn in 1877 where he set up a dry-goods business (a non-food general store) with his cousin Sussman, later persuading his seven brothers and sisters and his parents to join him in America.

Aaron Copland's mother, Sarah Mittenthal, was born in 1862 in Vistinich, Lithuania, only a few miles from the home of her future husband. In 1867 her father Aaron Mittenthal went to the United States where he set up a business as a store-keeper in Chillicothe, Illinois. His wife and family joined him in 1869; two years later they moved to New York City. Sarah possessed an attractive voice. It was her singing that first brought her to the notice of Harris Copland, and they were married in 1885.

Two years later Harris founded his own department store in Washington Avenue, Brooklyn, living on three floors above the store where their five children, Ralph, Leon, Laurine, Josephine and Aaron, all were born.

In an autobiographical sketch Copland wrote:

> I was born on a street in Brooklyn that can only be described as drab. It had none of the garish color of the ghetto, none of the charm of an old New England thoroughfare, or even the rawness of a pioneer street. It was simply drab. It probably

resembled most one of the outer districts of lower-middle-class London, except that it was peopled largely by Italians, Irish and Negroes. I mention it because it was there I spent the first twenty years of my life.[1]

The first musical influences on the young Aaron were the synagogue and domestic music-making.

My older brother [Ralph] played the violin to my sister's [Laurine] accompaniments, and there were passable performances of potpourris from assorted operas. I also remember a considerable amount of ragtime on top of the piano for lighter moments. But these were casual encounters. No one ever talked music to me or took me to a concert. Music as an art was a discovery I made all by myself.[2]

He began piano lessons with his sister Laurine as his mother and father were reluctant to pay for tuition:

My parents were of the opinion that enough money had been invested in the musical training of the four older children with meager results and had no intention of squandering further funds on me. But, despite the reasonableness of this argument, my perseverance finally won them over.[3]

At fourteen he received piano tuition at Leopold Wolfsohn's studio. His earliest serious attempts at composition were made when he had just reached his teens and he announced to a friend that he would like to be a composer. Indeed, he had written a song for his sister-in-law at the age of eight. He was fifteen when he attended his first concert, a piano recital by Paderewski at the Brooklyn Academy of Music.

In September 1917 he went to Rubin Goldmark for harmony lessons. Goldmark, a nephew of the composer Karl Goldmark and a pupil of Dvořák in New York, taught privately in Manhattan. He was totally out of sympathy with

---

[1] *The New Music 1900–1960* McGraw-Hill, New York, 1941 (revised edn., Macdonald, London, 1968), p. 151.
[2] *ibid.*, p. 151.
[3] *ibid.*, p. 152.

any modern music, putting the young Copland through a conventional theoretical training of counterpoint and composition according to classical precepts and forms. In the following months Copland became a piano pupil of Victor Wittgenstein. On graduating from the Boys' High School in 1918 he was able to devote more time to music. From the winter of 1919 to the spring of 1921 he studied the piano with Clarence Adler. His four years with Goldmark came to an end in 1921; of his teacher he said:

> Goldmark had an excellent grasp of the fundamentals of music and knew very well how to impart his ideas. I was spared the flounderings that so many musicians have suffered through incompetent training.[1]

Copland's first published work (excluding juvenilia), a *Scherzo Humoristique* for piano, subtitled *The Cat and The Mouse*, was completed in March 1919.

Over the years Copland had been saving money from the allowance his father had given him, supplemented by what he had earned in the store as relief cashier and for a brief period as a Wall Street Runner during the summer vacation. In 1919 his friend Aaron Schaffer, a Johns Hopkins graduate, had left America to study in Paris at the Sorbonne. His enthusiastic letters about musical life in the French capital soon fired Copland's imagination. Some time ago he had acquired a liking for French music: he had played Debussy's *Préludes* and pieces by Ravel. Performances of Debussy's *Nocturnes* by Stokowski and the Chicago Opera production of *Pelléas et Mélisande* with Mary Garden, presented in New York, had made a strong impression upon him. There was also in him a reaction against Goldmark's teaching on Germanic academic lines. France represented a freedom of expression, a liberating influence. The concerts of modern music in New York organised by the League of Composers and Edgard Varèse opened his eyes to the latest developments in European music.

In New York Copland had no soul-mates who thought as

[1] *ibid.*, p. 152.

he did. Salvation and stimulation could come only by a move to a different cultural environment. In *Musical America* he saw an advertisement giving details of the newly founded Summer School of Music for American Students to be established at the Palace of Fontainebleau in France in 1918. Instead of continuing at college Copland decided to go to France and was awarded one of nine scholarships to pay for three months' tuition at Fontainebleau.

Before he left America he was introduced by his cousin Elsie Abrams Clurman to her brother-in-law, Harold Clurman, who was soon to study literature at the Sorbonne. The two young men decided to share an apartment in Paris. In June 1921 Copland set sail for Europe on the liner 'France'. On the voyage he met the French artist Marcel Duchamp, who was to help him in Paris. They arrived at Le Havre on 16 June 1921 and one week later he enrolled at Fontainebleau.

Harold Clurman described the effect the next three years were to have upon the young composer:

> My friend Aaron Copland with whom I shared student days in Paris from 1921 through the summer of 1924 had become early in 1925 one of the season's musical celebrities. From these parties he used to bring back a kind of sizzling index of names that were hot in the Sunday supplements or the more exclusive weekly and monthly journals. All of these, he reported with a twinkling irony and some curiosity as to my reactions, were there.[5]

Copland became a pupil of Paul Vidal (1863–1931), whose attitude to music was conservative – not far removed from that of Rubin Goldmark. It was from another student at the Conservatory, a harpist called Djina Ostrowska, that Copland heard of Nadia Boulanger. In August 1921, after attending one of her classes, he began private lessons with her at 36 rue Ballu, in the Ninth Arrondissement. Copland's description of her provides a vivid portrait:

> In those early days she possessed an almost old-fashioned

[5] *The Fervent Years*, Dennis Dobson, London, 1946, p. 2.

womanliness that seemed quite unaware of its own charm. Her low-heeled shoes and long black skirts and pince-nez glasses contrasted strongly with her bright intelligence and lively temperament.[6]

Her powerful intellect also impressed him:

> Nadia Boulanger knew everything there was to know about music, pre-Bach and post-Stravinsky, and knew it cold. All technical know-how was at her fingertips: harmonic transposition, the figured bass, score reading, organ registration, instrumental techniques, structural analysis, the school fugue and the free fugue, the Greek modes and Gregorian Chant.[7]

She was particularly intrigued by her American pupil's familiarity with jazz. The notation of its complex cross-rhythms aroused her constant curiosity. The encouragement and constructive criticism provided Copland with the sympathetic intellectual stimulus he required.

> In my case she was able to extract from a composer of two-page songs and three-page piano pieces, a full-sized ballet [*Grohg*] lasting thirty-five minutes. True, no one has ever offered to perform the complete ballet, but the composing of it proved her point – I was capable of more than I myself though possible.[8]

After the First World War the musical centre of the world had moved from Vienna to Paris, where Ravel, Stravinsky, Satie, Roussel and Les Six were the leading figures. Just three days after his arrival in France, Copland had attended the premiere of Cocteau's ballet *Les Mariés de la Tour Eiffel*, for which the composers of Les Six (Milhaud, Honegger, Poulenc, Auric, Tailleferre and Durey) had jointly provided the music. At that event and at the first performance of Milhaud's ballet *L'Homme et son Désir* he had witnessed with amusement the reactions of a hostile Parisian audience.

[6] *On Music*, André Deutsch, London, 1961, p. 86.
[7] *ibid.*, p. 87.
[8] *ibid.*, p. 88.

In his 23rd year (photo courtesy of Aaron Copland)

And at Mlle Boulanger's apartment Copland saw all the leading musical personalities of the capital and met many now legendary literary giants, including James Joyce, Ernest Hemingway and Ezra Pound. Among the American composers who became his close friends were Virgil Thomson and Melville Smith, both Boulanger pupils, and George Antheil.

An important feature of Nadia Boulanger's teaching was the afternoon 'déchiffrage' seminars at first given to invited students but later opened to most of her pupils. On such occasions a wide range of music was studied and often performed. The assembled company might sing madrigals by Monteverdi and Gesualdo, two composers who until recently were enshrined in history books but seldom heard. Or the most recent works of Schoenberg and Stravinsky were closely analysed. In the early days, as Virgil Thomson described, after the session

> copious cakes were served and tea poured with frightening accuracy by the constantly trembling hand of Ma-

demoiselle's aged roly-poly and jolly mother, the Princess Mychetsky.[9]

Subjects beyond music were often discussed – contemporary art and literature, the latest works by Thomas Mann, Kafka, Gide, Pound. She possessed a close rapport especially with her American students.

What endeared her most to Americans was her conviction that American music was about to 'take off', just as Russian music had done eighty years before. Here she differed with the other French musicians, who though friendly enough towards Americans (we were popular then), lacked faith in us as artists.[10]

Although not one of her pupils, the American composer Ned Rorem said of her:

Nadia Boulanger, to everyone in the musical world and to thousands out of it, is the most remarkable pedagogue of our century, and perhaps (who knows) of all time.[11]

The new music of Paris encouraged Copland in his own compositions, as exposure to the works of Prokofiev, Stravinsky, Milhaud and Honegger opened up a new world with which he felt totally in sympathy. In conversation with Alan Blyth, Copland spoke of Stravinsky's influence:

I was affected by the whole rhythmic side of his music, also by its dryness, its non-Romanticism. He dominated the world of music at that time.[12]

His own music met with general critical acclaim. After the premiere of *Scherzo Humoristique: Le Chat et la Souris* (*The Cat and the Mouse*) by the composer at the Fontainebleau graduation concert on 23 September 1921 in the Salle Gaveau, Paris, Jacques Durand, the French publisher, offered to

[9] Alan Kendall, *The Tender Tyrant*, Macdonald and Jane, London, p. 58.
[10] *Virgil Thomson by Virgil Thomson*, Alfred A. Knopf, New York, Weidenfeld and Nicolson, London, 1966; republished by Da Capo, New York, 1977, p. 54.
[11] *The Paris Diary of Ned Rorem*, George Braziller, New York, 1966, p. 19.
[12] *The Times*, London, 14 November 1970.

issue the work. He paid an outright fee of 500 francs, approximately equivalent to $35 at the time. (Despite its French title, the *Scherzo Humoristique* had been completed in Brooklyn on 19 March 1920. His teacher Goldmark had been completely mystified by this novelty and felt unable to comment on it as he had no standards by which to judge it.) The piano writing shows a Gallic wit in the lightness of touch, distantly derived from Ravel's *Gaspard de la Nuit* and the Toccata from *Le Tombeau de Couperin*. For this, his first published composition, Copland produced an unconventional exercise in original craftsmanship. The spacing of chords towards the end is characteristic of the later works, with low bass notes in the left hand and idiomatic close harmonies in the right.

In the same concert Copland performed his *Sonnet III*, composed in 1920, and *Three Moods (Esquisses)*, unpublished until 1982, and he accompanied a Miss MacAllister in *Mélodie Chinoise*, subsequently retitled *Old Poem*. This song, to a text translated from the Chinese by Arthur Waley, was also a product of his days with Goldmark in Brooklyn and, as with the *Scherzo Humoristique* the influence of French impressionist music is evident.

After a second performance, by the American tenor Charles Hubbard and the composer on 10 January 1922 at a concert sponsored by the Société Musicale Indépendante in the Salle des Agriculteurs, Paris, *Old Poem* was accepted by another noted French publisher, Maurice Senart. A second song heard on that occasion, *Pastorale*, to words translated from Kafiristani by E. Powys Mathers, although composed in Brooklyn in April 1921, remained unpublished until 1979.

The first work from the Paris student days is a set of *Four Motets* on Biblical texts for *a cappella* chorus; they were completed in 1921 and performed at Fontainebleau under the direction of Melville Smith in 1924, but not published until nearly 50 years later.

Passacaglia

The Passacaglia for piano was begun in December 1921 and completed a month later. Its abstract nature and closely argued material were the products of Boulanger's rigorous musical discipline. Like the major keyboard works, the *Piano Variations* (1930), Piano Sonata (1941) and *Piano Fantasy* (1955–57), the emphasis on architectural structure is of overriding importance. It is based on an eight-bar theme in G sharp major (Ex. 1) and has eight variations.

Ex. 1

The classical form and contrapuntal devices applied to the piano have echoes of César Franck, whose influence as a teacher still pervaded the French scene, and the chromaticism of the second variation which takes the music to ever sharper keys would have received the approval of Franck. The doubling of the tempo for the fifth variation and the pause before the sixth variation break the cumulative unity usually found in a passacaglia. From the seventh variation to the end Copland builds up a powerful expansive grandeur that demands a virtuoso technique from the performer; here the music is at times written on three staves.

The composer was again fortunate to find a publisher soon after its composition; like *Old Poem* it was issued by Éditions Maurice Senart in 1922. Dedicated to Nadia Boulanger, it was first performed by Daniel Ericourt, a friend of Debussy, at the Société Musicale Indépendante in Paris in January 1923. The Passacaglia was accepted for a concert organised by the League of Composers in New York in November 1924 – with the *Scherzo Humoristique*, the first music by Copland to be heard in the United States. On 3 February 1931 it was presented as a ballet by Helen Tamiris with the title *Olympus Americanus*. Appropriately for a work in 'classical' form the scenario was set in ancient Greece. The music is divided into six parts: 'Basking in the Sun', 'Dance on an Ancient Theme (Priapic Ritual)', 'Tempo', 'Dance to Hermes and Aphrodite', 'The Races' and 'Triumphant'.

Rondino

The *Rondino* for string quartet (published as the second of *Two Pieces* for string orchestra) dating from early 1923 is thematically based (Ex. 2) on notes derived from the name of Gabriel Fauré, the Grand Old Man of French music, then approaching his 78th birthday. But despite its origin the music is more American than French in character. The division of the $\frac{1}{1}$ bar into $\frac{3}{8} + \frac{5}{8}$ produces a hint of jazz with occasional passages of polytonality.

Ex. 2

It was first heard at Fontainebleau in September 1924, two months before Fauré's death. The American premiere was given at an all-Copland concert in New York on 6 May 1928.

In July and August 1923, Copland and Harold Clurman spent the summer in Vienna, and from 2–7 August attended the first Festival of the International Society for Contemporary Music in Salzburg, a feast of new music where works by 54 composers were heard in the space of four days. Among the pieces that intrigued him were Alois Hába's Second String Quartet, which makes use of quarter-tones, Kodály's Sonata, Op. 8, for unaccompanied cello, and Ravel's Sonata for violin and cello. Also performed in the festival were Bartók's Second Violin Sonata, Schoenberg's song-cycle, *Das Buch der hängenden Gärten*, Stravinsky's *Concertino* for string quartet and a string quartet by the young and unknown William Walton.

As It Fell Upon a Day

In Vienna he completed an assignment Nadia Boulanger had given her class. She had required a piece for flute and clarinet but Copland added a solo voice, producing *As It Fell Upon a Day*, a setting of a poem by Richard Barnefield (1574–1627). Copland fulfilled his teacher's original instructions by writing imitative counterpoint for the two instruments in the introduction. The combination of two woodwind instruments and voice naturally produces a texture of ascetic severity.

Although the vocal line is a very free treatment of the madrigal text, the modal (mixolydian) harmonies and intervals of some passages provide an appropriate relationship to English music of the late 16th century.

At its premiere *As It Fell Upon a Day* impressed the audience and Paris critics. Raymond Charpentier wrote in *Commedia*:

> It shows a sensitive flexible nature and a technique which is already highly finished. With so few instruments a composer cannot bluff; he must play fair. Therefore every effort is doubly meritorious.[13]

It was performed again in Paris in a concert of American music on 5 May 1926. The American premiere took place in New York on 11 October 1935 in an all-Copland concert. The artists were Ethel and Otto Luening and Robert McBride – the two instrumentalists themselves composers of note in later years.

Grohg

The one-act ballet *Grohg* was inspired by his seeing a German horror film, *Nosferatu*, which is closely related to *The Cabinet of Dr Caligari*. To a scenario by Harold Clurman, *Grohg* concerns a vampire that sucks blood from dead bodies and that possesses the magic power to revive the dead and make them dance. Copland began the score under the guidance of Nadia Boulanger:

> Not that there was a company to commission it, or even choreographer. It was just that everyone was writing ballets at the time, and to do so became a must among the students. Under the enlightened dictatorship of Diaghilev, this genre was enjoying a powerful vogue. A student who might normally, in another milieu, write a symphony as his first big

[13] Quoted in Julia Smith, *Aaron Copland*, Dutton, New York, 1955, p. 61.

work, was likely instead to write some accompanying score
to a choreographic figment.[14]

From the score he extracted *Cortège macabre* (1923) and, at
the instigation of Nadia Boulanger, took it to Serge
Koussevitzky in his Paris apartment in the Spring of 1924. In
the presence of the conductor and Prokofiev, he played the
music on the piano. Koussevitzky, who had recently been
appointed conductor of the Boston Symphony Orchestra,
promised to include it in his first season, but this did not
happen and the first performance was given on 1 May 1925 by
the Rochester Philharmonic Orchestra under Howard Hanson.
The ballet, lasting 38 minutes, was completed in 1925 but it
has remained unperformed. Also from the original score of
Grohg Copland arranged three sections to form the *Dance
Symphony* which he entered for the RCA Victor Company
Prize in 1929, as he had not completed his *Symphonic Ode*, the
work he had intended to submit. He won a fifth of the prize
money, which was shared also by Louis Gruenberg and
Ernest Bloch, who each received $5,000 and Robert Russell
Bennett, who was awarded $10,000 for two works.

Dance Symphony
Although the Symphony for Organ and Orchestra was the
first of Copland's orchestral works to be performed, the
Dance Symphony should be considered his first in order of
composition, as the music was written between 1922 and
1925. The *Dance Symphony* employs a large orchestra,
including triple woodwind, piano and two harps. The
addition of two cornets to the brass section reflects the
influence of France, where composers from Berlioz to
Debussy have used these otherwise neglected instruments.
The extensive array of percussion has a definite American
flavour.

There is nothing in the music of the *Dance Symphony* that
specifically betrays its origin in a ballet. The strong rhythmical figures that abound in the fast movements are derived
from the thematic material itself and the separate
movements are in no way the episodic or 'mood' music which

[14] Quoted in Arthur Berger, *Aaron Copland*, OUP, New York, 1953, p. 9.

one might have expected from a score originally composed to accompany dance. The structure of the three linked movements is somewhat unusual, although these follow a fast-slow-fast pattern.

In the ballet the short slow introduction depicted the domain of the necromancer Grohg. A number of musical fragments and motifs that re-appear throughout the *Dance Symphony* provide a melodic unity for the thematic material in all three movements. In the opening bars (Ex. 3) the progression of triads on three muted trumpets repeat the interval of a third, usually a minor third, which can be traced in the harmonic and melodic material throughout the work.

Ex. 3

In the following *allegro*, 'Dance of the Adolescent', the fast tempo is not relaxed until the closing bars, *adagio molto*, which lead into the second movement, a slow waltz originally entitled 'Dance of The Girl Who Moves as if in a Dream'. The viola solo that links the slow movement to the finale makes an interesting use of quarter-tones, a daring experiment even for the early 1920s.

The last movement, 'Dance of Mockery', opens with a brilliant sprung rhythm in irregular metrical patterns (Ex. 4). This constituted the finale of the ballet where Grohg taunted his victims and servants. New material at fig. 29 maintains regular time-signatures but irregular accents. Copland's own essay on notation of irregular rhythms throws light on this problem and explains why he often altered bar-lines in revised works for ease of reading.[15]

Ex. 4

[15] *On Music*, p. 273 ff.

At fig. 38 the cross-rhythms between melody and accompaniment caused the composer to add an extra stave at the top of the score to indicate what the conductor should beat, a feature that is probably unique (Ex. 5). This is a curious and rather disturbing novelty as one assumes that the conductor beats according to bar-lines and time signature, not with the syncopation!

Ex. 5

The final orchestral *tutti* is an example of Copland's early mastery in combining four separate musical ideas that have appeared early in the movement into a coherent mixture of contrapuntal intricacy (Ex. 6). And the last chord with its semitone dissonance in the bass (Ex. 7) will be seen in later orchestral pieces as a characteristic 'trademark' of the composer in ending his works.

Ex. 6

Ex. 7

Despite the balletic origins of the *Dance Symphony*, it would be wrong to regard it as a ballet suite. The development of melodic and harmonic material both within each movement and throughout the work produces a composition that in

form and content is symphonic. The orchestration especially in the finale is functional rather than subtle. The
rhythmic drive in the fast movements is distinctly American
but the music remains cosmopolitan with no recognisable
national flavour.

II. Return to America
(1924–1928)

Shortly before Copland returned to the United States in June 1924, Nadia Boulanger was invited there by Walter Damrosch and Koussevitsky to appear as solo organist with the New York Symphony Orchestra and the Boston Symphony Orchestra respectively. Her confidence in the young American prompted her to ask him to write a work for her to play. Copland accepted the commission

> despite the fact that I had written only one work in extended form before then, that I had only a passing acquaintance with the organ as an instrument, and that I had never heard a note of my own orchestration.[1]

Organ Symphony

Copland began composing his Symphony for Organ and Orchestra in the Summer of 1923 while staying at Milford, Pennsylvania, where he was earning a living playing the piano in a hotel trio. It is surprising that under these conditions he was able to complete the whole score by the Autumn of the same year. As with the *Dance Symphony*, Copland used a large orchestra: triple woodwind, full brass (but no cornets), and an array of percussion requiring six players in addition to the timpanist. The Symphony is in three movements, although the opening Prelude is merely an introduction to the second movement, a Scherzo, which takes on more significance than in most symphonies, acting as the powerful centre of the work.

The principal theme on a solo flute in the first bars (Ex. 8) introduces the interval of a third, providing a reminder of the *Dance Symphony*, where the same interval is an integral feature of the whole work. The motif on the strings accompanying the entry of the organ also relies on a minor third. Copland's economical use of material allows him to derive

[1] *The New Music 1900–60*, p. 156.

all the thematic development from the opening flute melody.

Ex. 8

The Scherzo maintains a strong rhythmical drive from beginning to end with one brief interruption of slower music. There is no clear 'theme' as such; all the melodic material derives from the pervading ostinato set at the beginning of the movement. Many of these passages are built up from irregular groupings of notes with uneven accents which disregard the bar-lines.

The climax before the central Trio and its return at the end of the movement with the full force of brass and percussion is Copland at his most ferocious. It is little wonder that the New York audience at its premiere was overwhelmed by the work. The finale is more restrained emotionally; in a way that must have pleased Mlle Boulanger, the movement is a passacaglia in form but with only the first three notes being present at each repetition. The separate variations are usually based not directly on the theme itself but on the preceding derivation of it. Bars 5 to 8 of the theme are a variant of bars 1 to 4 with certain intervals widened but the overall shape of the phrases is maintained (Ex. 9). In the succeeding thirteen sections, the

Ex. 9

theme undergoes the customary contrapuntal treatment, in canon, diminution and augmentation with varied counter-figures. Copland's invention makes this no mere technical exercise: the development of the music is compact, avoiding episodic fragmentation. The result is a powerful expression of Copland in what he termed his 'European' voice. The role of the organist is partly that of a soloist, partly a member of the orchestra; the passages when the organ is unaccompanied are brief. At other times it blends into the orchestral texture, but very little of the organ part doubles the instruments. Nevertheless the work is a symphony, not a concerto.

As promised, on 11 January 1925 Nadia Boulanger played the Symphony with the New York Symphony Orchestra under Walter Damrosch in Aeolian Hall, New York City. After the performance, the conductor, unusually, turned to remark to the audience: 'If a young man at the age of 23 can write a symphony like that, in five years he will be ready to commit murder'. One critic described the Symphony as a 'new and seething crater'. A second performance, in Boston on 20 February of the same year, was the beginning of a valuable friendship between the composer and Koussevitzky. Copland began to write music to suit the characteristics of the Boston Symphony Orchestra with their particular sound in mind. Virgil Thomson describes the impact of the work upon him:

> When [Nadia Boulanger] asked me how I liked it, I replied that I had wept. 'But the important thing,' she said, 'is why you wept.' 'Because I had not written it myself,' I answered. And I meant that. The piece was exactly the Boulanger piece and exactly the American piece several of us would have given anything to write and that I was overjoyed someone had written.[2]

With simple exactitude Harold Clurman described Boulanger's reaction to New York:

> About that time Copland and I accompanied Nadia Boulanger on her first walk up the Great White Way [Broadway]. It was really ablaze in those days, you remember, and not without a certain pride I asked 'what do you think of it?' 'It is extraordinaire, but not very raffinated,' she answered.[3]

[2] *op. cit.*, p. 71.
[3] *op. cit.*, p. 3.

At a Chicago performance in 1934 the critic Claudia Cassidy wrote:

> It begins with a reverie, breaks into a squalling scherzo and ends, screaming like a bewildered banshee which by some twist of locale has found itself at the wailing wall.

First Symphony

In 1928 Copland made a version of the Organ Symphony which replaced the part for organ with additional orchestration. While retaining the original instruments he added alto saxophone, four horns, two trumpets, piano, tom-tom and glockenspiel. The organ part was allocated to the woodwind in lyrical passages and to the piano in the orchestral *tutti*. Otherwise the distribution of music among the orchestra remains substantially unchanged. The additional brass comes into its own in the massive organ chords in the closing bars of the Finale. This is not a revision in the sense that the second version of the *Symphonic Ode* is a revision, because even after four years, Copland saw no need to alter the structure or material in any way. For some inexplicable reason there is a change of rehearsal letters in the second version. To distinguish the two works, Copland called the original 'Symphony for Organ and Orchestra' and the later one 'First Symphony'. The First Symphony was completed in 1928 and premiered by the Berlin Symphony Orchestra under Ernest Ansermet in Berlin in December 1931. The Scherzo in this version had been performed by Fritz Reiner and the Philadelphia Orchestra in Carnegie Hall, New York, on 4 November 1927. Looking back after many years Copland wrote:

> For a while I thought of the Organ Symphony as being too European in derivation and in the works that followed – in *Music for the Theatre* of 1925 and the Piano Concerto of 1926 I felt I had come closer to a specifically American idiom. In retrospect, however, I saw that the jazzy scherzo, for instance, points to the works that were to follow, and also that the Symphony generally was closer to my natural expressive idiom than I had realised.[1]

[1] Sleeve notes to the CBS recording of the Organ Symphony, MS 7058.

Otto Deri has written: 'American music dates from Copland's return from Paris to the States in 1925. His importance lies in the fact that he gave direction to the country's musical life'.[5]

Two Choruses

In January 1925 Copland composed two choruses for female voices, the first unaccompanied, the second with piano. They were performed on 24 April of that year in the Engineering Building, New York City, by the Women's University Glee Club conducted by Gerald Reynolds, with the composer playing the elaborate piano accompaniment to the second chorus. The first, *The House on the Hill*, is a setting of a text by the American poet, Edward Arlington Robinson (1869–1935), from his anthology *Children of the Night* (1897). It opens with a wordless vocalise divided antiphonally between two female choruses that recurs throughout the piece to emphasise the melancholy, lamenting nature of the poem which describes Robinson's own abandoned home:

> They are all gone away
> The House is shut and still
> There is nothing more to say
> Through broken walls and gray
> The winds blow bleak and shrill,
> Nor is there one today
> To speak them good or ill.

The vocal writing is in close imitation, further evidence of the composer's strict neo-classical musical education. The melodic lines follow Phrygian and Lydian modes. There are no common bar-lines; instead each voice part has vertical lines dividing the phrases to indicate the stresses of the words. The independence of the four parts has the appearance on paper of a 14th-century motet, further emphasised by the modal shapes of the melodic lines. The result is however more than an exercise of academic counter-point: it is an expressive setting of deliberate simplicity.

In contrast the second chorus, *An Immorality*, is a

[5] *Exploring 20th Century Music*, Holt, Rinehart and Winston, New York, 1968, p.170.

sophisticated, jazzy song for solo soprano, SSA chorus and piano. The text is a poem by Ezra Pound (whom Copland had met in Paris) from *Lustra*, published in 1916. *An Immorality* is a work of considerable rhythmical and polytonal complexity. The alternating major/minor thirds and the vamping accompaniment of the piano in $\frac{3}{4}$ against $\frac{1}{1}$ in the voice part look back to the scherzo of the First Symphony and forward to the Piano Concerto of the following year. In spirit and character this chorus is close to the American popular songs of the 1920s, epitomised by Gershwin.

This was Copland's first wholly characteristic 'American' work; the melodic, harmonic and rhythmical features owe nothing to Europe. The piano writing is totally derived from jazz and the popular music of his own country.

In October 1925 Copland was the recipient of the first Guggenheim Fellowship awarded for music. The sum of $2,500 allowed him to devote himself solely to composition for the ensuing year, and the Fellowship was renewed for a further year until 1927.

Music for the Theatre

Koussevitzky's faith in Copland was confirmed when within a month of the premiere of the Organ Symphony he persuaded the League of Composers to commission a work for a concert he was to conduct for the League in the following season. *Music for the Theatre* (Copland prefers the English spelling) was begun in May 1925 in New York and continued during the summer at the MacDowell Colony in Peterborough, New Hampshire. It was completed in September at a summer school organised by his former piano teacher Clarence Adler at Karinoke on Lake Placid. The suite of five movements has no specific literary or dramatic associations. Copland's own introduction provides a succinct description of the work:

> The composer had no play or literary idea in mind. The title simply implies that at times this music has a quality which is suggestive of the theatre.

> 1. Prologue (*Molto moderato*; $\frac{2}{1}$). The first theme is

announced almost immediately by the solo trumpet. Shortly, this gives way to the entrance of the strings, who gradually form a background for the oboe singing the second theme. A short development follows (*allegro molto*), built upon a transformation of the first trumpet theme. After a quickly attained climax, there is a return to the first part and a quiet close.

II. Dance (*Allegro molto*; $\frac{5}{8}$). This is a short, nervous dance, with form and theoretic material so simple as to make analysis superfluous.

III. Interlude (*Lento*; $\frac{1}{4}$). The interlude is a kind of 'song without words' built on a lyric theme which is repeated three times, with slight alterations. The English horn solo plays an introductory phrase, and then to an accompaniment of strings, piano and glockenspiel, the main theme is sung by a clarinet.

IV. Burlesque (*Allegro vivo*; $\frac{3}{8}$). The form of this movement is best expressed in the formula A–B–A–B. For the rest, this Burlesque is best explained by its title.

V. Epilogue (*Molto moderato*; $\frac{1}{1}$). No new themes are introduced here. Material from the first and third parts only is used. The quiet mood of the Prologue is recaptured and the work ends *pianissimo*.

Copland uses a small theatre orchestra: single woodwind, two trumpets, trombone, percussion (but no timpani), piano and a small body of strings. The writing for trumpets with both jazz and orchestra mutes, and for percussion, virtually a dance-band kit, is very close to jazz. The jazz elements and polyrhythms of the *Dance Symphony* and *An Immorality* are even more evident in *Music for the Theatre*. The repeated notes on the trumpet beginning slowly, *senza misura*, becoming faster and faster, closely resemble the oboe theme at the beginning of the Scherzo of the *Dance Symphony*; the two-note ostinato that accompanied it appears again in the *allegro* of the Prologue to the *Music for the Theatre* (Ex. 10). The cross-rhythm of the woodwind theme is closely related in character to melodic figures in the Scherzo movements of both the earlier Symphonies.

Ex. 10

In this same movement Copland suggests an alternative rebarring of the woodwind passage to accommodate the different rhythms of melody and an accompaniment, similar to the additional stave for the conductor in the finale of the *Dance Symphony*. The lyrical writing in the Interlude for solo woodwind and strings recalls the slow movement of the *Dance Symphony* both melodically, harmonically and in scoring.

The 'Burlesque', as the title suggests, is an example of the composer's laconic wit and lively humour, brilliant and irreverent at the same time.

Throughout the work Copland avoids counterpoint, concentrating upon melody and accompaniment as the principal features. Considered by many to be one of his most important compositions, *Music for the Theatre* is totally American. Koussevitzky conducted the premiere at Symphony Hall, Boston, on 20 November 1925, and a week later it was heard in New York. The more conservative critics were unimpressed by its modernism. Other performances followed at the Paris Opéra in the spring of 1926 again under Koussevitzky, at the ISCM Festival of 1927 in Frankfurt, in Mexico City under Carlos Chávez on 3 February 1929, in Philadelphia with Stokowski on 2 April 1932 and twice more in Mexico City on 2 September 1932, and at the Festival of Pan-American Chamber Music held there in July 1937.

In 1926, in the company of Harold Clurman, Copland returned to Paris for six months. He renewed his friendship with Nadia Boulanger and met Roger Sessions for the first time, and in July of that year he visited the ISCM Festival in Zurich. This proved less of an historic occasion than the inaugural Festival of 1923 in Salzburg, but several important works were heard, including Hindemith's

Paris, 1926, in Nadia Boulanger's flat. From left: Virgil Thomson, Walter Piston, Herbert Elwell and Aaron Copland, before a concert of their music (photograph by Thérèse Bonney).

Concerto for Orchestra, Schoenberg's Wind Quintet, Walton's Overture *Portsmouth Point*, Webern's *Five Orchestral Pieces*, Op. 10, and the Violin Concerto of Kurt Weill. Copland reported on these concerts for *Musical America*.

Two Pieces

From this time date Copland's *Two Pieces* for violin and piano, 'Nocturne' and 'Ukulele Serenade'. The Nocturne is dedicated to his fellow composer Israel Citkowitz (1909–1974), also a Boulanger pupil. As with the *Rondino* for string quartet, the time-signature is divided as $\frac{3+5}{8}$ Copland's favourite interval, a minor third, at first rising, later falling, dominates the opening *Lento moderato* (Ex. 11). The three-note figure (a) in bar 3 is repeated in almost every bar of the whole piece. The contrasting central *Meno mosso (Grave)* introduces a new figure, but this too ends with the falling minor third on the three-note figure (Ex. 12). The coda, a compressed repetition of the *Grave*, ends with a combination of the three-note figure and the minor third. Copland's typical economy of harmony and melody is seen here at its most concise.

Ex. 11

Ex. 12

The companion piece, 'Ukulele Serenade', is dedicated to Samuel Dushkin. The opening *vivo* is in the composer's jazzy vein with added-sixth chords for the piano, *glissandi* and quarter-tone inflexions in the violin line (Ex. 13). The relaxed second part introduces the 'ukulele' with quiet arpeggiated chords on the piano accompanying the serenading melody on the violin. As in the chorus *An Immorality*, bar-lines for the two instruments do not coincide. Later the roles are reversed when the *pizzicato* quadruple stoppings of the violin represent the ukulele accompanying the piano. The music of the opening returns to provide a coda of brilliant virtuoso display for the two performers.

Ex. 13

Piano Concerto

On 12 February 1924 George Gershwin had surprised the
musical world at a concert in the Aeolian Hall, New York,
with his *Rhapsody in Blue*. It was followed in 1925 by his Piano
Concerto in F, the first idiomatically American concerto for
the instrument.

In the late summer of 1926, Copland and Harold
Clurman spent three months at Guethary in the Basses
Pyrénées before returning to America in October. There he
worked on his Piano Concerto, completing it in New York
before the end of November. Although possessing jazz
features, it differs fundamentally from Gershwin's work.
The aggressive nature of the second movement with its
uncompromising dissonances is far removed from the bland
charm of *Rhapsody in Blue* and the Concerto in F.

Copland employs an orchestra on a scale similar to those
of the two previous symphonic works: triple woodwind with
the addition of E flat clarinet and saxophone, full brass,
extensive percussion and strings. The Concerto is cast in
two linked movements. As with the *Dance Symphony* and First
Symphony, Copland begins with a slow introduction, not too
distant from Gershwin in rhapsodic mood. The opening
three-note figure is integral to the whole work and is heard
sixteen times within the first eight bars in a dove-tailed
pattern of questions and answers between the strings and
brass (Ex. 14). Most of the material is treated canonically

Ex. 14

with cross-rhythms in the contrapuntal interplay. When
there is a passage of such intricacy in melodic writing as Ex.
15, the accompaniment maintains a regular pattern in each
bar. This can be compared to the beat of a jazz band against
which the solo instruments syncopate. The pervading
interval of a minor third and the slow tempo give a blues
feeling to the music. In several places the piano part is
written on three and four staves to clarify the distribution of

notes and phrases. The brief coda neatly sums up the ideas in the compact movement, by presenting the melodic material again in the clearest and simplest manner.

Ex. 15

The second movement bursts into activity with a wild, sardonic jazzy piano·solo, ranging over the entire keyboard in a kind of cadenza. It opens with a motif (Ex. 16) derived from the three-note figure of the first movement. In the tenth bar there is a rapid *accelerando* to twice the speed (Ex. 17). This is the closest approximation the composer can give to the jazz rhythms which the pianist actually plays. As is the custom in jazz, the rhythm ♩♪♫♪ ♫♪♫♪ is played almost as ♩♪ ♩♪ ♩♪ ♩♪. Similarly what Copland has notated as ♫♫♫♫ is to be performed as a cross between what is written and ♩♪ ♩♪.

Ex. 16

Ex. 17

Throughout these solo bars, the left hand plays an ostinato that is almost a parody of the customary left hand of the jazz pianist, with its mixture of single bass notes to determine the harmony, alternating with a spread chord at least an octave higher. Later, in addition to the jazz in the piano part, Copland creates a jazz band within the orchestra itself. The piano vamps a tonic-dominant accompaniment to a soprano saxophone, piccolo, E flat clarinet, muted trumpet and muted trombone which each in turn have solo 'breaks'. The addition of a side-drum played with a brush and a Chinese drum completes the band.

With its jazzy dance-rhythms, this movement looks ahead to the ballets *Billy the Kid*, *Rodeo* and *Appalachian Spring* with many bars of vigorous accompaniment and little or no melody. There is none of the ingratiating qualities of Gershwin in Copland's Piano Concerto, and its forceful character alienated both critics and audiences. Philip Hale of *The Boston Herald* commented: 'We found little to attract, little to admire, much to repel'. Only Lawrence Gilman in *The New York Herald Tribune* had a kind word for the work. He described it as having 'a fullness and authenticity of life which makes it at once perturbing and richly treasurable'. Others were roused to anger. Samuel Chotzinoff in *The New York World* of 4 February wrote:

> The jazz there was a pretty poor pick, as those things go. But Mr Copland surrounded it with all the machinery of sound and fury, and the most raucous modernistic fury at that. The composer-pianist smote his instrument at random: the orchestra, under the impassioned baton of Mr Koussevitzky, heaved and shrieked and fumed and made anything but sweet moans until both pianist and conductor attained such a climax of absurdity that many in the audience giggled with delight.

The editorial in *The Boston Evening Transcript* of 5 February described the work as 'a harrowing horror from beginning to end. There is nothing in it that resembles music except as it contains noise'; and Paul Sanborn, writing in *The New York Telegram* (4 February 1927), saw in the Concerto 'gargantuan dance movements as a herd of elephants engaged in jungle rivalry of the Charleston and dances further south.'

Copland's parents, who had travelled to Boston for the performance, were much disturbed by the hostile reception of the critics. But at the New York premiere a week later, the audience was more enthusiastic. After the Piano Concerto (which is dedicated to Alma Morgenthau, who had become his patron upon his return to the U.S. from Europe in 1924) Copland turned away from jazz as a significant element in his compositions.

During the composition of the Concerto, Copland produced two short piano solos, *Sentimental Melody (Slow Dance)*, originally entitled *Blues No. 1*, and a separate *Blues*, eventually published as the last of the *Four Piano Blues* (pp. 117–119).

On 10 April 1927 Copland was one of the pianists in the notorious concert in Carnegie Hall of music by George Antheil at which his *Ballet Mécanique* created a sensation equal to that caused by the Paris premiere in the previous year. In late April 1927 Copland again went to Europe for several months, where in Paris on 30 May he attended the premiere of Stravinsky's *Oedipus Rex*, conducted by the composer. At the end of June he travelled to Frankfurt for the ISCM Festival at which his *Music for the Theatre* was performed. Later at the Baden-Baden Festival of German Chamber Music he much admired Alban Berg's *Lyric Suite*.

Poet's Song

His own exposure at this time to music of the twelve-note system produced one short serial work composed in Königstein, near Bayreuth, originally entitled *Song* but later renamed *Poet's Song*, a setting of a poem by E.E. Cummings. It is based on the note-row in Ex. 18. The repeated phrase in the piano and the contours of the melodic line imply modulating tonality rather than serial chromaticism. Only in the last two bars where the opening music is speeded up is all sense of key dispelled. In some respects an experimental piece, it was not performed until October 1935.

Ex. 18

On his return to New York after the summer Copland took up a lecturing post vacated by the critic Paul Rosenfeld at the New School for Social Research; his association with that institution lasted for nearly ten years. And with Roger Sessions he organised the Copland-Sessions Concerts of Contemporary American Music held from 1928 to 1931, in which works by American composers constituted the principal items in the programme.

Lento Molto

Copland's next published compositions were the *Two Pieces* for string orchestra. The second of these, *Rondino on the Name of Gabriel Fauré*, had been written in 1923 and played in the original version for string quartet at Fontainebleau in September 1924.

The first, marked *Lento molto*, was also composed firstly for string quartet between February and April 1928. It is homophonic throughout, with the melodic lines harmonised by parallel triads that recall New England hymnody with a Stravinsky-like astringency and economy of means. The only feature in common with the *Rondino* is the canonic treatment of the slowly unfolding thematic material.

The first performance of the *Two Pieces* together for string quartet was given by the Lenox Quartet at the second Copland-Sessions concert at the Edyth Totten Theatre, New York, on 6 May 1928. During August and September 1928, staying at the MacDowell Colony in New Hampshire, Copland arranged them for string orchestra. In this version they received their premiere in Symphony Hall, Boston, on 14 December 1928 conducted by Koussevitzky.

Vocalise

Professor A.L. Hettish of the Paris Conservatoire was the editor of a series of 100 vocalises – wordless vocal exercises – published by Leduc in ten volumes. Gabriel Fauré had provided the first of the set in 1907. Aaron Copland was asked for a contribution which became No. 71 in the series. The vocal line in the first part of *Vocalise* (Ex. 19) comprises

Ex. 19

scales alternating with a chorale-like sequence of longer notes. The central section leading to a cadenza is a long cantilena of expressive simplicity. At one point Copland introduces the scales of the opening of the work, producing his familiar combination of two time signatures. The piano part, confined predominantly to the treble stave, is very spare, providing only a modest support for the voice. This attractive work is not a mere vocal exercise but deserves a place in any recital with 'standard' songs.

Beginning in October 1927, Copland presented twelve public lectures, mainly on modern music, thereby establishing firmly his role of lecturer and writer alongside his increasing reputation as a composer. In addition to an opening 'General Survey' and a concluding summary, he spoke on ten major compositions: *Boris Godunov* (Mussorgsky), *Pelléas et Mélisande* (Debussy), *Das Lied von der Erde* (Mahler), *Daphnis et Chloé* (Ravel), *Pierrot Lunaire* (Schoenberg), *The Rite of Spring* (Stravinsky), *Prometheus* (Scriabin), *La Création du Monde* (Milhaud), *Das Marienleben* (Hindemith) and *Oedipus Rex* (Stravinsky).

After performing his Piano Concerto in Hollywood Bowl on 20 July 1928 under Albert Coates, Copland visited the composer Henry Cowell in San Francisco who agreed to publish *As It Fell Upon a Day* in the New Music Edition he had founded.

II. Abstract Music

(1928–1935)

Copland's experience of playing in a hotel trio after his return to the United States in 1925 left some slight marks on the Piano Concerto and the *Two Pieces* for violin and piano, with their hints of jazz and popular music. By 1928 such influences had for the most part disappeared, even when the instrumental medium might have sparked off an unconscious memory.

Vitebsk

The Piano Trio *Vitebsk* of 1928–29 is a rare example of Copland's inspiration from Jewish music. The folk theme on which the work is based was heard by the composer during a performance of Solomon Ansky's play *The Dybbuk*,[1] presented by the Moscow Arts Theatre at the Neighborhood Playhouse in New York City. The folksong itself had been noted down by Ansky in his home town of Vitebsk, whence the title for the Piano Trio.

The introduction (Ex. 20) combines a two-note figure in

Ex. 20

---

[1] In 1974 Leonard Bernstein also used Ansky's play as the basis for his ballet *The Dybbuk*.

the strings using quarter-tones with harshly dissonant major/minor triads on the piano. The cello then introduces the Jewish theme which is treated canonically with the violin (Ex. 21).

Ex. 21

The central section is a fast Jewish dance, the Hora, beginning with running quavers on the strings and right hand of the piano over a four-note ostinato in piano, left hand (Ex. 22). The succeeding semiquavers in violin and

Ex. 22

piano suggest wild gypsy fiddle music. The middle part of the dance fragments the music into three- and four-note patterns derived from the principal theme exchanged between the three players. The return of the dance, now even more frenzied, incorporates an altered version of the folk theme; an abrupt interruption of the activity is followed by a recapitulation of the complete theme in grand style on the violin and cello with Russian bell-like sonorities for the piano. A repetition of the opening bars marks the coda as the music becomes less assertive. And a final statement of the theme on the cello leads to the closing bars that leave the bitonality unresolved.

Here as in earlier works, Copland reveals an economy of thematic material. Except for the folk melody and central dance, he uses principally two-, three- and four-note motifs. The piano texture is characteristically lean, with his customary use of low bass notes, ostinati in the left hand and wide spacing of percussive chords where the hands are often more than two octaves apart.

The establishment of the Cos Cob Press in February 1929 provided American composers with a music publishing venture prepared to issue new works, especially orchestral scores and parts, with no regard for their commercial success. Copland's patron Alma Morgenthau was president – she provided the financial backing – and Edwin F. Kalmus, later to become an independent publisher, was the manager responsible for the business side of the organisation. Existing publishers in the United States were rarely willing to take risks with new works, and Copland's own good fortune with publishers in Europe was seldom shared by others. Cos Cob accepted most of his unpublished scores: *Dance Symphony*, Symphony No. 1, *Music for the Theatre*, Piano Concerto, *Vitebsk* and later *Poet's Song* and the *Piano Variations*. Cos Cob merged with Arrow Music Press in 1938 but maintained the same altruistic basis whereby composers received half the money from sales instead of the usual 10%. Arrow Music issued the *Two Pieces* for string orchestra in 1940. (Both catalogues were later taken over by Boosey and Hawkes in 1956.) With financial support from his New York patron, Copland went to Paris in 1929 to promote a concert of American music. On 17 June five composers were represented on the programme: Virgil Thomson, Roy Harris, Israel Citkowitz, Aaron Copland and Carlos Chávez, all but the last former pupils of Nadia Boulanger. The pieces performed were:

Virgil Thomson: *Quelques Airs*

Roy Harris:	Sextet for clarinet, piano and string quartet
Israel Citkowitz:	*Three James Joyce Songs*
Aaron Copland:	*Vitebsk*
	Two Pieces for String Quartet
Carlos Chávez:	Piano Sonata

The concert was well received by audience and critics alike.

Symphonic Ode

To celebrate the 50th anniversary of the Boston Symphony Orchestra in 1930, ten composers were commissioned to write works, only Ravel failing to fulfil the request. The others produced symphonic compositions of major significance:

Aaron Copland:	*Symphonic Ode*
Howard Hanson:	Symphony No. 2, *Romantic*
Edward Burlingame Hill:	Symphony No. 2 in C
Paul Hindemith:	*Konzertmusik* for strings and brass
Arthur Honegger:	Symphony No. 1
Sergey Prokofiev:	Symphony No. 4
Ottorino Respighi:	*Metamorphoseon*: Theme and Variations
Albert Roussel:	Symphony No. 3
Igor Stravinsky:	*Symphony of Psalms*

Copland had begun the *Symphonic Ode* as early as 1928. Although the score was completed in 1929, it was not performed until 19 February 1932 under the baton of Koussevitzky in Boston and repeated in New York. The *Ode* was also heard later that year on 18 November in Mexico City by the Orquesta Sinfonica de México, Carlos Chávez conducting. The composer explained in a programme note that the title *Symphonic Ode* 'is not meant to imply any connection with a literary idea. It is not an ode to anything – other than the particular spirit to be found in the music itself. What that particular spirit is, is not for me to say'.

The original score called for a very large orchestra, including eight horns, five trumpets, and two tubas. In the revised version of 1955, the orchestral forces are still on an extensive scale: quadruple wind, four horns with an optional further four, four trumpets, piano, two harps, and four percussion players who cover twelve instruments. At first the Boston Symphony Orchestra players found difficulty in following the alternating time-signatures, and the conductor suggested that in certain passages the notation should be altered to facilitate the reading of complex rhythms.

Many years later, in a tribute to the conductor who was to become his most enthusiastic proponent, Copland gave the following account of their difficulties:

> Koussevitzky informed me that the orchestra had spent several hours rehearsal on the *Ode* and still could not play it. He suggested that if I changed the $\frac{2}{4}$ and $\frac{6}{8}$ section to $\frac{5}{4}$ the men could probably play it without any trouble. I laughed at the notion that this was a difficult rhythm and told Koussevitzky that there was nothing to it – the rhythm is an easy one to play. He immediately replied: 'Come on up to Boston, take over the rehearsal yourself and you'll find out how "easy" it is. After an hour's rehearsal, we can play about three bars,' he jokingly concluded.
>
> Since I was reluctant to make any change in the score, I went to Boston to attend the next rehearsal. Koussevitzky turned the orchestra over to me and left the hall. We went through the piece and I was convinced the rhythm was difficult for them. Thereupon I agreed to do as the conductor wished and changed the whole section to read $\frac{5}{4}$.

After a further performance of the original version conducted by Thor Johnson at the Juilliard School in 1949, Copland decided to revise the *Symphonic Ode*. He himself gave the following explanation:

> The revision was undertaken primarily for the following reasons:
> 1. To reduce the size of the orchestra, mainly for practical reasons.
> 2. Some of the rhythms had caused considerable performance difficulties in the thirties, and these have been notated differently. They still are not child's play but an attempt has been made to simplify performance

        problems while at the same time retaining the original rhythmic patterns.

3. Certain pages in later perspective, seemed needlessly bony in structural outline. These were filled in with fuller textures.

4. The opening and closing sections of the original were written quite high for brass and strings. These have been lowered somewhat with concomitant re-adjustment in the tonality scheme.

5. Only at one point were completely new measures substituted for those of the original. Those occur at the start of the $\frac{7}{4}$ section that leads to the apotheosis of the end.

6. Before the first performance, a cut of approximately three orchestral pages had been made towards the end of the slow section. About two of those pages have now been restored.

Since the original manuscript version has been withdrawn, we must assume that, apart from the alterations mentioned above, the work in its present form is substantially unchanged.

With the *Symphonic Ode*, Copland moved away from a direct use of jazz, but preserved many of its more vital characteristics, especially those of rhythm. Copland has explained his motives in doing so:[2]

> With the [Piano] Concerto, I felt I had done all I could with the idiom, considering its limited scope. True, it was an easy way to be American in musical terms, but all American music could not possibly be confined to two dominant moods, the 'blues' and the snappy number. The characteristic rhythmic element of jazz, being independent of mood, yet purely indigenous, will undoubtedly continue to be used in serious native music.

This work also marks the beginning of Copland's austere rhetorical style, seen most clearly later in the *Short Symphony*, the *Orchestral Variations* and *Connotations*. The word 'bony' that the composer used to describe part of the *Symphonic Ode* is the most apt adjective for the angularity of melody and

[2] *The New Music 1900–1960*, p. 151.

starkness of harmony. Copland offered his own succinct analysis of the *Symphonic Ode*:

> As a whole, the work is cast in five-sectioned form that can be represented as roughly ABCBD. Sections A, C and D are slow tempo, section B in fast tempo. The massive opening section A gradually acquires momentum and breaks up into the 'feathery brightness' of the allegro section B, which is followed by C, a more lyrical treatment of the first section's material. The repetition of the allegro B is only approximate. It moves imperceptibly into section D which combines A and B to form a coda in the monumental mood of the opening.

Basically, the *Ode* is in sonata form; in characteristic manner, Copland presents all the significant thematic material in the opening bars. The first rhetorical theme, on two trumpets and two trombones in octaves, comprises four phrases, each of four or five notes, punctuated by an emphatic answer from the remaining wind instruments, cellos and double basses (Ex. 23 *a*, *b*, *c* and *d*). This answer itself is derived from the octave interval in the principal theme. The phrase *d* in Ex. 23 is a quotation from the *grave* section of the 'Nocturne' of 1926. These epigrammatical

Ex. 23

phrases contain all the elements of the entire work. Throughout, Copland makes considerable use of wide spacing in melodies, and the arpeggio feature of phrases *a* and *b* and the interval of an octave. Throughout the massive opening section with heavy orchestration, Copland, with his customary economy, derives all the melodic material directly from the above theme, not yet developing it, but instead making extensive use of canon and augmentation, with fragments of the phrase dovetailed with each other in a closely knit pattern of continually moving crotchets. For 60 bars this crotchet/minim movement is maintained without a single quaver in any part. A gradual increase in tempo over 62 bars takes the music from *Largamente* (♩ = 60) to *subito allegro* (♪ = 162). This use of an *accelerando* spread over a number of bars appeared in the Piano Concerto but the change there to double the speed was accomplished in 17 bars (second movement: figures 14 to 16). The section which follows, denoted B in Copland's own analysis, is built on three- and four-note figures closely related to the opening theme. The irregular rhythmic phrases are punctuated by percussion, in a display of nervous exchanges between woodwind and strings. In Copland's symphonic design this represents his scherzo. The melodic outlines (Ex. 24) are clearly derived from the first theme. In the succeeding

Ex. 24

section from figure 19 this grouping of quavers into irregular patterns of two and three is again featured but here the rhythm is in 'unison', not one against the other. Thus in the fifth bar of figure 19 all the parts have the rhythm shown in Ex. 25. Throughout this *allegro*, from figures 19 to 30 (for a

Ex. 25

total of 124 bars), the music maintains this 'unison' rhythm at all times; every instrument moves in the same rhythm with

virtually no counterpoint. Bar-lines serve the same purpose
that they do in madrigals: they help to indicate simultaneous
movement of parts in the score, but only occasionally are
they an indication of accent. The indulgence of the full
orchestra for as many as four whole pages of score in the
dancing rhythm of Ex. 26 looks forward to *El Salón México* and

Ex. 26

$\frac{3}{4}$ ♪♩ ♩ ♪ | $\frac{3}{8}$ ♫♩ | $\frac{5}{4}$ ♩ ♩ ♩ ♪ ♫♫ |

Danzón Cubano, which have similar repeated rhythms for long
passages of heavy orchestration. At figure 28 the music
becomes more fragmented and material from previous
episodes returns. Section C, which Copland describes as a
more lyrical treatment of the opening music, appears after a
pause, restoring the tempo of the beginning *lento e drammatico*.
First violins and horns present in canon a lyrical melody
from phrases *d* and *a* (Ex. 27).

Ex. 27

The sudden return of the *allegro* (figure 38) is no mere
repetition of the earlier music, but a further development of
it in a similar manner. At figure 45, *più mosso, molto ritmico*
(♩ = 208, another example of Copland's high metronome
marks), the timpani establish a *basso ostinato* of intervals
derived from the opening theme, which closely parallels the
coda of the finale of Symphony No. 1. The relaxation of the
tempo leads into the closing section D, *Lento maestoso* (figure
52), where the principal themes of Sections A and B are
combined. He ends the *Symphonic Ode* as he began, with a
massive unison statement of the opening theme. The final
bar is a firm and unambiguous chord of B flat major with the

pervading upward leap of an octave on piccolo, oboes, piano and first violins.

Copland regards the *Symphonic Ode* as one of his most important works: 'I tried for something there; I tried hard; and I feel that I succeeded in what I attempted'. Critical response was unenthusiastic although not entirely hostile. Only H.T. Parker of *The Boston Evening Transcript* expressed approval:

> There is no mistaking the power of the introductory and the final divisions. The one strives and ascends. The other calms and deepens. Into the slow division enters the severer beauty of our day and of this new music, which is the beauty of metal in motion.

Even Lawrence Gilman of *The New York Herald-Tribune*, who had previously supported the composer, condemned the work in uncompromising terms:

> It was my pleasure and privilege to praise Mr Copland's widely execrated Piano Concerto when it was played five years ago. But in comparison with that gusty and joyously challenging work, the new *Ode* is, for the most part, impotent and unrewarding. Hearing it, one visions Mr Copland lost in agonizing lucubration, praying heaven to make him Hard and Stripped and Sharp-Edged and Astringent and all other things that a composer must learn to be in order to escape the sin of sensibility.

Despite the composer's high regard for the *Symphonic Ode* and the improved critical view of the work by present-day writers, the work has been performed seldom and remains with the Organ Symphony and *Short Symphony* among his neglected major compositions. Julia Smith admirably sums up the character and quality of the *Ode*:

> Highly individual in respect to its melodic and polyrhythmic design, Jewish in respect to its grandeur and prophetic note, and French in its craftsmanship, the *Symphonic Ode* stands out as the most distinguished and compelling work of the first period.[1]

[1] *op. cit.,* p. 118.

The Depression, which had such a profound influence upon writers and film-makers, seems to have created little permanent effect upon the musical scene. Although Copland's family were members of the Democratic Party, he himself never subscribed to any political group. He did however show sympathy towards the wave of liberal feeling that swept through the artistic world in particular. The immediate results of the Wall Street Crash produced a drastic reduction in activities in the musical field. Concerts and lectures became less frequent and commissions for new works dwindled. In January 1930, Copland went for six months to Bedford, New York. Financially secure there for a while with the RCA Victor Symphonic Award of $5,000 for the *Dance Symphony*, he worked on the *Piano Variations*. At the invitation of Mrs Elizabeth Ames he spent the summer of 1930 at Yaddo, Saratoga Springs, New York, where he conceived the plan for a Festival of American Music. On 9 August he returned briefly to New York City to perform the Piano Concerto at the Lewisohn Stadium under Albert Coates, who had conducted the work at the Hollywood Bowl in 1928.

Piano Variations

The *Piano Variations* of 1930 mark a new direction towards absolute music. The rhythmical complexities and pungent harmonies are an extension of the language in the *Symphonic Ode*. Although critical opinion now considers the *Variations* a masterpiece, the spare texture and fragmentary melodic features were at first so disconcerting that the significance of the work was not apparent. It introduced a radically new ascetic style that eliminated the earlier influence of jazz; gone too is diatonic melody and harmony and the lyricism of the Piano Concerto and First Symphony.

In his study of Copland, Arthur Berger states that as an example of conciseness, we could scarcely find anything better than the *Variations*. As with the *Symphonic Ode*, the composer confines the initial material to five notes. This 'restricted row' serves for all the variations with remarkable economy, ingenuity and craftsmanship in an uncom-

promising, declamatory manner. Copland asserts[1] that the
theme of the *Variations* which opens the work (Ex. 28) is
really the first variation.

Ex. 28

In spite of its apparently unique character, this theme
contains a number of traits common to Copland's melodies
in other works of the 1920s and 1930s. The phrases are of
four and five notes each (*cf.* the *Symphonic Ode*); the second
phrase is almost an exact repetition of the first, with the
addition of one note (E) and the alteration of note-values;
the theme is entirely in minims and crotchets (*cf.* the
Symphonic Ode and First Symphony: third movement), and
incorporates intervals of major sevenths and minor ninths
as a prominent feature (*cf.* the *Dance Symphony*). In bar 8
there is a widely spaced arpeggio, which is used extensively
in the succeeding variation (*cf.* the *Dance Symphony*, First
Symphony, Piano Concerto, *Symphonic Ode*, *Short Symphony*).
The interval of a third, of such significance in the *Dance
Symphony* and the First Symphony, is also an important
characteristic of the melody, since it opens each of the four
phrases. The unusual spacing of chords with seconds and
thirds low in the bass and the clusters of closely packed
notes in the interjectory chords have appeared in the piano
parts of earlier works.

The variations follow as a continuous chain so that often

[1] *What to Listen for in Music*, p. 93.

the transition from one to the next is aurally imperceptible. This is achieved by retaining some common element of rhythm or melodic pattern as a link. In each variation, every chord and figure can be traced back directly to the theme. In Variation I the original melodic leaps of sevenths and ninths are transposed an octave to produce a line that moves mostly by step (Ex. 29).

Ex. 29

As in earlier works, development of the material arises through canonical treatment, the alteration of rhythm and tempo and fragmentation. Echoes of previous compositions are clear: for example, Variation VII presents an outline reminder (Ex. 30) of the opening of the *Symphonic Ode*.

Ex. 30

The retention of four- and five-note figures and the frequent changes of time-signature look forward to the *Short Symphony* of 1933. These similarities are even more evident in his orchestration of the *Variations*, which dates from 1957. The irregular rhythmic patterns of Variations XIV to XVI (especially the alternation of $\frac{3}{8}$, $\frac{2}{8}$ and $\frac{7}{8}$) recall Bartók's piano pieces on Bulgarian dances, which possess the same nervous energy.

The coda is in Copland's characteristic slower majestic style, so that the massive chords of the close resemble the final passage of the First Symphony, but also seem to look ahead to the grinding dissonances of *Connotations*, a work composed thirty-one years later but significantly only four years after the *Orchestral Variations*. The last four bars resort to four staves, using the third, sustaining pedal of a Steinway grand if available. An alternative notation is given for pianos which do not have this facility. This is further evidence of the composer's use of the instrument to its full potential for producing a wide range of effects.

In conversation with Leo Smit at Harvard University on 1 November 1977 during a 'Learning from Performance Program', Copland revealed:

> The *Variations* somehow filled a special niche in my production. I think it was one of the first works where I felt that 'This is me' – that somebody else taking the same theme, would have definitely written something different. That's only natural, but in my mind, the piece had a certain 'rightness' about it. The *Variations* seemed to flow one after another – varied of course, each one different – but each one seemed to follow on the other.[5]

The critic of *The New York Times* commented that the composer 'has been attracted more and more to the "stream of consciousness" school and more than one passage yesterday recalled similar essays in words of Gertrude Stein'. Jerome D. Bohm, writing in *The New York Herald Tribune*, said: 'Mr Copland, always a composer of radical tendencies, has in these variations sardonically thumbed his nose at all of those esthetic attributes which have hitherto been considered essential to the creation of music'. And Wilfrid Mellers says of the work: 'The Variations embrace all the physical and nervous energy of city life. If it has the hardness of the New York skyline, it has also the sense of new vistas'.[6]

Miracle at Verdun

At the beginning of 1931, Copland provided incidental music for Hans Chlumberg's play, *Miracle at Verdun*. The Theater Guild production was staged in the Martin Beck Theater, New York City on 16 March 1931.

During April 1931, in the company of Paul Bowles, Copland went to Europe, visiting Paris, Berlin and London,

[5] The full text of this conversation is printed as Appendix 1 on pp. 197–212.
[6] *Music in a New Found Land*, Barrie and Rockliff, London, 1964, p. 86.

where the ISCM Festival was being held. Gershwin's *An American in Paris* and Sessions' First Piano Sonata, performed in Oxford, were the representative works from the United States. For these concerts, Copland acted as the correspondent for *Modern Music*. In Paris he visited Gertrude Stein who persuaded him to go to see North Africa, and so, after spending May and June in Berlin and the short stop in London, the two men travelled to Morocco for a three-month stay.

Back in Berlin in December, Copland organised a concert of American music conducted by Ernest Ansermet. The programme included the first performance of Copland's First Symphony in the version of 1928 without organ, Sessions' First Symphony, *Portals* by Carl Ruggles and the *Jazz Suite* by Louis Gruenberg. This concert offered the first serious music by American composers to be heard in Germany since the previous century. In London on 16 December, Copland presented a concert of chamber music by American composers. He performed his own *Piano Variations* and a Sonatina by Carlos Chávez; also in the programme was a Sonata for oboe and clarinet by Paul Bowles. In late December he returned to New York.

The First Yaddo Festival of American Music took place at Saratoga Springs, New York, in April 1932. The size of the auditorium, which could seat only 200 people, limited the programme to chamber music. 18 composers were represented by 35 works. Again Copland played the *Piano Variations* and the reaction from both critics and audience was enthusiastic.

Through the summer of 1932 he worked on two new pieces, the *Short Symphony* and *Statements* for orchestra. At the end of August, in response to an invitation from Carlos Chávez, Copland undertook a five-month visit to Mexico. Chávez had already conducted *Music for the Theatre* and the First Symphony in Mexico City and planned an all-Copland concert for 2 September. On that evening at the Teatro de Orientación were heard the *Two Pieces* for string quartet, *Piano Variations*, the choruses *The House on the Hill* and *An Immorality* and *Music for the Theatre*. The *Piano Variations* appeared with *An Immorality* in another concert on 22

September, and on both occasions his music created a strong impression. Chávez conducted the *Symphonic Ode* on 18 November in Mexico City.

The colourful, exotic atmosphere of Mexico deeply influenced Copland, producing not only the overtly Mexican pieces of later years (*El Salón México* and *Three Latin-American Sketches*) but also affecting his use of irregular rhythms of dance and the brilliance of orchestration. During the Mexican sojourn he composed two *Elegies* for violin and viola, commissioned by the League of Composers and performed in New York on 2 April 1933 but subsequently withdrawn. He also continued to work on the *Short Symphony* and *Statements*.

Short Symphony

The *Short Symphony* was completed in 1933 and first performed in Mexico City on 23 November 1934 under Chávez, to whom it is dedicated. Although it was scheduled for performance in the United States on several occasions, it was found rhythmically too taxing for the players. Not until 1944 was it heard in America, in a radio broadcast by the NBC Symphony Orchestra conducted by Stokowski. Even as late as 1962 it was to have been performed in London by the composer and the London Symphony Orchestra, but was withdrawn before the concert through insufficient time to prepare it adequately.

The problems of performance led the composer to make an arrangement of it in 1937 as a Sextet for clarinet, piano and string quartet, and in this form it has been heard more often. Although the original music remains unchanged, except for the removal of the last two chords, certain bar-lines and time-signatures are altered in an attempt to simplify the notation of complicated rhythms.

The scoring of the *Short Symphony* is for medium-sized orchestra without timpani, percussion and trombones but including the almost obsolete heckelphone which doubles with the cor anglais and can be replaced by that instrument if necessary. The *Short Symphony* is cast in three movements: an opening *allegro vivace* – for the first time an important movement and not merely an extended introduction, as in the previous Symphonies and the Piano Concerto; an elegiac *Lento*, notably simple in comparison to the outer movements; and a fast finale.

Initially there seems to be little in common between this Symphony and the previous symphonic works. The lyricism has been replaced by a brittle toccata-like quality with scant evidently melodic interest. A careful examination reveals that most of Copland's characteristics of composition are still present although the outward style is different. Its nearest musical relatives are the *Piano Variations* and *Statements*, the latter of which he was composing at the same time.

A curious feature of the first movement is that the opening 82 bars are entirely in unison except for the punctuating chords and a brief passage of two-part counterpoint near the beginning. Like the *Symphonic Ode*, the germ of the first movement lies in the opening two bars. All the melodic figures that appear in the rest of the movement are derived from this short figure (Ex. 31). The sequence of notes is 'serial' in character, comprising a nine-note row.

Ex. 31

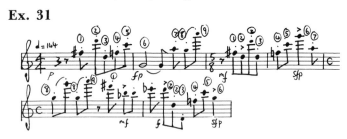

Again as in the *Symphonic Ode*, the opening melody consists of five- and six-note phrases, separated each time by interruptions on other instruments; this is heard even more clearly in the version for sextet. As in previous works, the rhythmical impulse is produced by the pattern of quavers in irregular groups of two and three. Two characteristics in Copland's melodic writing are evident in almost every bar: the use of arpeggios and wide leaps, often, as in the *Symphonic Ode*, of two octaves.

As similarly in the Piano Concerto, the first movement is joined to the second by a short bridge passage. The nervous rhythmical energy gives way to a continuous flow of tranquil melody; the rush of irregular quavers is transformed into a sequence of slow minims. At one point (fig. 25) in the middle of the movement, the slow and inevitable unfolding of melody over an ostinato bass has an affinity with Stravinsky's *Symphony of Psalms,* which (like the *Symphonic Ode*) was composed a few years earlier for the 50th anniversary of the Boston Symphony Orchestra.

The finale is similar in character to the first movement. The dancing rhythms look forward to *El Salón México* and *Appalachian Spring.* The melodic figures are based on wide intervals and arpeggios. Without relaxing the tempo, Copland introduces a contrasting passage in minims (Ex. 32), based on the opening notes of the whole work but recalling the mood of the slow movement.

Ex. 32

In this way, the musical ideas of all three movements are related to provide the appropriate unity. In a letter to the composer, dated 1 December 1934, Chávez wrote:

> The dialectic of this music, that is to say, its movement, the way each and every note comes out from the other as the *only* natural and logical possible one, is simply unprecedented in the whole history of music. The work as a whole, I mean to say in its entirety, is an organism, a body in which every piece works by itself 100% but whose mutual selection is such, that no one part can possibly work and exist without the other. There has been much talk about music in which everything is essential, nothing superfluous, but as far as I know, *the talk* about such music exists; yes, but not the music itself. The 'Little Symphony' [*sic*] is the first realization of this I know of, and yet the human content, the inner expression is purely emotional. It is precisely that tremendous human impulse which made possible such realization.

Let me tell you what I thought when I got the Little
Symphony – well here is the real thing, here is our music,
here is my music, the music of my time, of my taste, of my
culture, here it is, a simple and natural fact to myself, as
everything belonging to oneself is simple and natural. [7]

Although the *Short Symphony* may never achieve the
popularity of Copland's ballets, its craftsmanship and logic
produce increasing admiration on repeated hearings. As an
abstract composition, it is a masterpiece of compact
invention. The economy of material and relevance of all
melodic and rhythmical development typify the composer's
musical mind.

Into the Streets May First

Copland's one overt excursion into politics was his setting
of a poem by Alfred Hayes, *Into The Streets May First*. With it
he won first prize in a competition organised by the
Communist-controlled Composers' Collective for a May-
Day song in 1934. It was published in the magazine *New
Masses* in May 1934 and in the *Workers' Songbook 2* (1935).

What success it may have achieved seems to have been
short-lived. After this, his attempts to reach the people
through his music turned away from ideological paths
towards the wider and less controversial area of folk music,
without political overtones.

Hear Ye! Hear Ye!

Copland spent the summer of 1934 at the holiday bungalow
of his cousin Leo Harris on the edge of Lake Bemidji,
Minnesota. There he completed the score of a ballet for
Ruth Page, *Hear Ye! Hear Ye!* The premiere was given at the
Chicago Grand Opera on 30 November 1934 as one of four
short ballets. The scenario is set in a law court during a
murder trial. Making use of dance music and jazz, the score,
still unpublished, contains much parody, with reference to
the Mendelssohn Wedding March, among other quotations.

---

[7] Reprinted in *Letters of Composers*, ed. Gertrude Norman and Miriam Lubell
Shrifte, Greenwood Press, Westport, Connecticut, 1979, pp. 393–4.

From February to June 1935, Copland taught at Harvard in place of Walter Piston, who was on leave of absence. In conversation with Edward T. Cone, he explained why he had never accepted a permanent university appointment:

> One of the reasons I never thought about teaching in a university is that I had no degree. I graduated from high school and decided not to go to college in order to devote all my time to music. I didn't have the requirements I supposed one needed to teach in a college.[8]

Statements

Statements was completed in New York City in June 1935. Commissioned by the League of Composers, it was intended for performance by the Minneapolis Symphony Orchestra but at its premiere only the last two movements were presented in an NBC broadcast on 9 January 1936 by that orchestra under Eugene Ormandy. Not until 7 January 1942 was the complete work given when Dimitri Mitropoulos conducted the New York Philharmonic Orchestra in Carnegie Hall. In a programme note for the first performance Copland wrote:

> The title 'Statement' was chosen to indicate a short terse orchestral movement of a well-defined character lasting about three minutes. The separate movements were given suggestive titles as an aid to the public in understanding what the composer had in mind when writing these pieces.

Their titles are 'Militant'; 'Cryptic'; 'Dogmatic'; 'Subjective'; 'Jingo'; 'Prophetic'.

'Militant' employs the full orchestra, with the omission of clarinets, although there is a part for bass clarinet. It opens with a powerful unison theme incorporating Copland's usual features of wide intervals and arpeggios. A further Copland characteristic in these bars is the punctuation of each phrase by brief answers on the brass (*cf.* the *Symphonic Ode*). As in previous works the separate phrases of four and five notes are inter-related and developed by canonic

[8] *Perspectives on American Composers*, ed. Benjamin Boretz and Edward T. Cone, W.W. Norton, New York, and Princeton University, 1971, p. 143.

fragmentation. Like the opening of the *Symphonic Ode* the
notation is entirely in crotchets and minims. The harmonic
texture is typical of earlier compositions: similar bitonality
between the upper orchestral range and the bass line has
appeared frequently before.

The second movement, 'Cryptic', is scored for wind
instruments: flute, bass clarinet, bassoon and brass. Its title
is perhaps derived from the ambiguous tonality of the
melodic lines (Ex. 33).

Ex. 33

Harmonically there is a relationship between this
movement and the first. The conflicting tonalities in Ex. 34
are close to several passages in 'Militant'.

Ex. 34

The closing bars, like the opening, are still unresolved
harmonically. Although the separate melodic phrases are
diatonic, it is unclear which key has been reached.

The third *Statement*, 'Dogmatic', is an *allegro* with no real
theme, only a five-note figure (Ex. 35) which persists
thoughout the movement. The reiterated pattern at fig. 2
(Ex. 36), with its inability to escape the punctuating chords,
emphasises the dogmatic stubborn mood. At fig. 3, with a
slight relaxation of the tempo, horn and trumpet between
them interpolate the theme of the *Piano Variations* in chorale-
like long notes. It is difficult to determine any particular
significance in this direct quotation unless this pattern of
notes still obsessed the composer. The final exorcism to lay
the theme to rest comes in 1957 with the *Orchestral Variations*.

Ex. 35

Ex. 36

The fourth *Statement*, 'Subjective', is scored for *divisi* strings without double-basses. Like the previous movements, it is monothematic; the three phases presented on the first violins are closely related to each other. Development arises from canonical treatment and the alteration of intervals.

The fifth *Statement*, 'Jingo', is a rondo for full orchestra. The title and music suggest a parody of 1920 dance music and is a rare example of where Copland's musical training in France is evident. The witty satirical style has something in common with pieces written at this time by Poulenc and Milhaud, and at one point (fig. 3, bar 6) the theme and accompaniment has the flavour of Stravinsky's Suites in its hurdy-gurdy orchestration. The tune is based on 'The Sidewalks of New York', a political campaign song of the time. 'Jingo' opens with two brief phrases (Ex. 37) that constantly recur throughout the movement. The 'theme' itself comprises chromatic one-bar phrases, hinted at by trumpet and oboe, and eventually given a full statement on the bass clarinet (Ex. 38).

Ex. 37

Ex. 38

It is interesting to note that Copland retains the same time-signature throughout the movement even where rhythmic patterns do not follow bar lines. Generally orchestral players find complex cross-rhythms easier to read if the time signature does not alter from bar to bar except where absolutely necessary. Bitonality appears in this movement in a passage where the bass-line is in G major while the upper parts are firmly in D flat major, the most alien key possible. In the climax which follows, the accompaniment is locked into 18 bars of the same repeated chord against which the brass and upper wind present anarchic outbursts of conflicting figures and tonalities. Without slackening the pace, Copland fragments the music, allowing it to fade away into *pppp*.

The sixth and last movement, 'Prophetic', is an ominous slow movement with contrasts of violence and lyricism. The unifying element is the series of repeated notes presented in almost every bar. Each of the opening three phrases (Ex. 39) consists of a number of repeated crotchets, ending with a rise or fall of a third onto a sustained note. The repeated dissonant chords are built on intervals of fourths and ninths (*cf.* the repeated chords of 'Jingo').

Ex. 39

The coldness and emptiness of the musical picture of the future drawn so far is changed by a trumpet melody marked *cantabile, dolce nobilmente* (Ex. 40) which emerges like a ray of warm hope amidst the desolation that has gone before. The slow procession that closes the movement (and work) moves through a passage of mixed tonality, and the trumpet melody re-appears to provide a conclusion of serene beauty rare in Copland's works.

Ex. 40

Reviewing the first complete performance, Virgil Thomson wrote:

> These highly personal pieces show Copland at his best, and that means being one of the most direct of living music writers and one of the most amiable of men.[9]

Statements (1935) represents the last work in a series of abstract compositions from *Symphonic Ode* of 1929 and continuing with the *Piano Variations* (1930) and the *Short Symphony* (1933). Although at present they remain overshadowed in popularity and frequency of performance by the ballets and other later orchestral pieces, their importance in the composer's development cannot be over-emphasised. The musical public of the time may have encountered difficulties in coming to terms with them owing to their uncompromising qualities. Fifty years later, these problems should no longer arise. The clarity of conception and musical language offer no barriers to audiences who now readily accept the major works of Bartók and Stravinsky which at first seemed so alien.

[9] *The New York Herald Tribune*, 8 January 1942.

IV. American Consciousness: i
(1935–1942)

During the early 1930s Copland began to voice doubts about the relationship between the composer and the musical public. In an autobiographical essay he wrote:

> . . .I began to feel an increasing dissatisfaction with the relations of the music-loving public and the living composer. The old 'special' public of the modern music concerts had fallen away, and the conventional concert public continued apathetic or indifferent to anything but the established classics.
>
> It seemed to me that composers were in danger of working in a vacuum. Moreover, an entirely new public for music had grown up around the radio and phonograph. It made no sense to ignore them and continue writing as though they did not exist. I felt it was worth the effort to see if I couldn't say what I had to say in the simplest possible terms.[1]

What Do We Plant?, Sunday Afternoon Music & The Young Pioneers

A response to these views is seen in the three short pieces for children written in the summer of 1935 while the composer was at the MacDowell Colony in Peterborough New Hampshire. The first, a song for two-part chorus and piano, *What Do We Plant?*, to a text by Henry Abbey was composed at the request of the Henry Street Music School in New York and performed by the Girls' Glee Club. He contributed two easy pieces to an educational series of piano music by contemporary composers edited by Isadore Freed and Lazare Saminsky and published by Carl Fischer: *Sunday Afternoon Music* and *The Young Pioneers*.

El Salón México

Copland's first work to gain world-wide popularity, *El Salón*

---

[1] *The New Music 1900–60*, p. 160.

México, was a direct product of his visit to Mexico in 1932. At the dance hall 'El Salón México' in Mexico City he heard native Mexican folk music which, with its asymmetrical rhythms and brilliant colouring, provided the initial inspiration for his own work.

El Salón México is scored for the orthodox full orchestra, although the composer indicates that the cor anglais, E flat clarinet, bass clarinet, contra-bassoon and third trumpet can be replaced if necessary by other instruments in the orchestra. The percussion includes a gourd, chinese block and a cymbal played with a brush.

Copland gave the following explanation of the motive behind the work:

> No doubt I realised even then that it would be foolish to attempt to translate into musical sounds the more profound side of Mexico: the Mexico of the ancient civilizations or the revolutionary Mexico of to-day. In order to be able to do that, one must really know the country. All that I could hope to do was to reflect the Mexico of the tourists; because in that 'hot spot' one felt, in a very natural and unaffected way, a close contact with the Mexican people. It wasn't the music that I heard, but the spirit that I felt there, which attracted me. Something of that spirit is what I hope to have put into my music.[2]

The themes he uses (Ex. 41) he did not in fact hear in the dance hall; he took them from two collections of folk melodies: Frances Toor's *Cancionero Méxicano* and Ruben M. Campos' *El Folk-lore y la Música Méxicana*.

The introduction, derived from 'El Palo Verde' ('The Green Stick'), leads to a solo trumpet cadenza based on 'La Jesusita' ('The Little Jesus'). As the music increases in tempo, bass clarinet and bassoon present a modification of the third melody 'El Mosco' ('The Fly'), answered in the violins on a similarly varied version of 'El Palo Verde'. In the principal *allegro vivace* (fig. 11) Copland develops all these themes by alterations of rhythm and combining phrases from the separate melodic figures of the original

---

[2] In the miniature score published by Boosey and Hawkes, 1939.

Ex. 41

tunes. The opening arpeggio figure recurs throughout this section as a unifying element. Where possible regular time signatures are maintained for ease of reading, although the additive rhythms (Ex. 42) pose initial difficulties of

Ex. 42

syncopation. In a brief respite from the headlong rush to the middle of the work, a *Moderato* (fig. 19) introduces a clarinet solo which has its remote origin in the second strain of 'El Mosco'. And the gradual return to the original tempo introduces two further variants of the original melodies that seem at first new themes. Closer scrutiny (Ex. 43) reveals that each has its relationship to 'La Jesusita'. The closing

Ex. 43

(b)

section re-introduces material of the main section in different order and in different keys, with a coda based on the
opening bars.

The first performance, in a version for two pianos by John
Kirkpatrick, was given by him and the composer at the New
School for Social Research in New York on 11 October 1935.
The orchestral version completed in the following year
received its premiere in Mexico City by the Orquesta
Sinfónica de México under the direction of Carlos Chávez.
It was well received by critics and audience alike. They
recognised that the flavour of the music had the same
qualities as works by their own composers, especially
Chávez and Silvestre Revueltas.[3] The short melodic figures,
asymmetrical rhythms and 'primitive' orchestration using
Mexican percussion clearly possessed national characteristics. Performances in London at the ISCM Festival in
June 1938 and in Paris during the following year marked
the beginning of Copland's international popularity. The
recording made by Koussevitzky and the Boston Symphony
Orchestra brought the music to audiences throughout the
world, and led Boosey and Hawkes to offer the composer
a long-term contract to publish all his compositions.

Might Copland be accused of compromising his artistic
integrity in his desire to reach a wider public by simplifying
his style? The adoption of folk-material to this extent is new
to Copland, although he was making use of it in *The Second
Hurricane*, his opera for school children on which he was

---

[3] Revueltas (1899–1940) was a Mexican conductor and self-taught composer of
colourful orchestral music using national dance rhythms. His short but active life –
he was also a violinist, teacher, political activist and champion of new music – was
cut short by alcoholism and a poverty that had already claimed the lives of two
daughters. Virgil Thomson, writing in *The New York Herald-Tribune* of 4 March 1941
(reprinted in *A Virgil Thomson Reader*, Houghton Mifflin, Boston, 1981, p. 213 – an
excellent collection of Thomson's varied and vigorous prose), described Revueltas'
music as 'both racy and distinguished. . . .The model is a familiar one of the
nationalist composer whose compositional procedures are conservative and
unoriginal but whose musical material consists of all the rarest and most beautiful
melodies that grow in his land'.

occupied at this time. In most other respects he had not abandoned his former principles. The melodic figures are mostly
triadic with the familiar arpeggio motifs. Harmonically
and rhythmically he is intrinsically the same: the irregular
metres with misplaced accents, polytonality arising from
melodies in one key, accompaniment in another. The
frenetic energy of the fast sections and lyricism of the slow
still have much in common with the preceding orchestral
works, especially the *Short Symphony* and *Statements*.

*Copland with Nadia Boulanger and Serge Koussevitzky in Symphony
Hall, Boston, photographed by Victor Kraft in the 1940s.*

The Second Hurricane

Towards the end of 1935, Copland was asked by Grace
Spofforth, Director of the Music School of the Henry Street
Settlement in New York, to compose a stage work for
high-school children. Edwin Denby provided the libretto of
this 'play-opera for school performance', entitled *The Second
Hurricane*, and Copland began work on the music early in
1936.

The story is set in the 1930s with no particular location, although vaguely in the Southern Mid-West. Six high-school children become marooned when their aeroplane, carrying relief supplies to the scene of a hurricane and flood, is forced to land. The threat of another hurricane forces them to overcome their individual conflicts and to unite in a heroic effort of working together.

Most of the score was completed during the summer of 1936 when Copland and Denby were staying in Tlaxcala, Mexico. The opera was first performed in April of the following year, when the producer was Orson Welles. Naturally, the music is in a deliberately simple form appropriate for untrained voices, but, as with the works Benjamin Britten composed for children, there is no writing down for the performers. In conversation with Lawrence Gilman, the composer confessed:

> I wished to be simple to the point of ordinariness. This was comparatively easy in relation to the more colloquial passages of the libretto where the music approaches musical operetta, but in the more dramatic moments, it was rather difficult to make the distinction between grand opera and high school opera.[4]

The vocal writing mostly comprises short repeated phrases, but with sufficient character to be memorable. Often the chorus is in unison, or thirds, with simple canonic figures. Copland's melodic trade-mark, the interval of a third, is much in evidence. The first two numbers, both choruses of the 'grown ups', are good examples. Ex. 44 gives the first.

Ex. 44

Although the concerted items probably have the strongest impact in performance, it is the solo songs which possess the most marked individuality. Gyp's song in Act 1, although brief and comprised of only one phrase, repeated

[4] Lawrence Gilman, 'An Opera for School Children to Sing', *New York Herald-Tribune*, 4 April 1937.

five times with slight alteration, has a haunting quality.
Note here the ubiquitous interval of a third in Ex. 45.

Ex. 45

The most extensive continuous music appears in Act 2. A
chorus, 'Two Willow Hill', leads to a sextet for the children,
again built mostly on the interval of a third. From the sextet
emerge two solos, the first for Jeff, a negro boy who joins the
students. Copland sets his words to a jazzy accompaniment
of 'blues' thirds and syncopation.

'Queenie's Song' looks forward to the lyrical music of
Copland's heroine Laurie in his second opera, *The Tender
Land*, of some twenty-five years later. The hint of bitonality
between the voice and accompaniment (Ex. 46) gives the

Ex. 46

folk-song melody a Coplandesque flavour. And the scene
ends with the six principals singing 'The Capture of
Burgoyne', an American Revolutionary song taken from the
Harris collection of *American Poetry and Plays*, issued by Brown
University, Providence, Rhode Island. This marks
Copland's first use of an American folk-song in one of his
works. The lively orchestral part with its dancing rhythms
and perky instrumentation gives a preview of what is to
come in the three 'American' ballets. In other respects there

are reminders of earlier scores, *Music for the Theatre* and *Statements* in particular.

The Second Hurricane was the first important work by an American composer to be written specially for children. The result is well within the capability of high school pupils and is doubtless fun to sing, although open to question are the naivety of the plot and an ingenuous morality that might prove unacceptable to children today. Much of the linking dialogue is pedantic and unrealistic, and even the fragments preserved on the recording of 1960 are spoken by the performers with acute embarrassment and little conviction.

Prairie Journal (Music for Radio)

In 1936 the Columbia Broadcasting System commissioned *Music for Radio* for broadcast performance by its radio orchestra. It was one of several works in the network's first American Composer's Commission series. Written during the following year, it was performed under its original title on 25 July 1937 by the Columbia Broadcasting Symphony Orchestra under Howard Barlow. Other composers who provided works at this time were Louis Gruenberg, Howard Hanson, Roy Harris, Walter Piston and William Grant Still. CBS also organised a competition for a subtitle for *Music for Radio*: the winning entry, from a Miss Ruth Leonhardt of Grosse Pointe, Michigan, was *Saga of the Prairie*. In 1968 it was retitled *Prairie Journal*. The score is dedicated to Davidson Taylor, director of the Music Section of the Columbia Broadcasting System.

The music is cast in a single movement lasting 12½ minutes and is scored for the normal full orchestra with the addition of two saxophones and vibraphone. As with later Copland orchestral works, the piano is an important member of the percussion. In characteristic dance-band style, trumpets and trombones are instructed to use different kinds of mute. The mood is similar to that of the incidental music for plays and films which occupied Copland during the next three years. The language is simple with ostinato figures and folky melodies. The second theme (Ex. 47) presented on a solo clarinet has a description 'simply, in the manner of a folk-song'.

Ex. 47

Unlike previous orchestral scores but following closely the character of *The Second Hurricane*, composed at the same time, *Music for Radio* is well within the capability of an amateur orchestra. Gone are the intricate irregular rhythms and technically demanding passages. That the orchestral parts are available on sale in the Youth Orchestra Series is a clear indication that the publishers have non-professional performances in mind. It is one of the few pieces not yet recorded under the direction of the composer. And although a minor creation beside the more impressive earlier scores, presenting Copland in nostalgic vein (as the subtitle implies), it is the most substantial single-movement orchestral piece of the non-symphonic works.

In 1937 Copland became Chairman of the Board of the newly founded American Composers' Alliance, remaining its President until 1945. This organisation sought to protect the performing rights of music by American composers. The Executive Board included Marion Bauer, Roy Harris, Goddard Lieberson, Douglas Moore, Quincy Porter, Wallingford Riegger, Elie Siegmeister, Roger Sessions and Bernard Wagenaar.

Billy the Kid
In addition to *Grohg*, which remained unperformed, and *Hear Ye! Hear Ye!*, Copland's music had been used for two other ballets at this time: *Olympus Americanus* (1931), based on the Passacaglia for piano, with choreoraphy by Helen Tamiris, and *Dithyrambic*, produced by Martha Graham in New York in 1932 to the *Piano Variations*. The first of his popular ballets, *Billy the Kid*, was composed in Paris and Peterborough, New Hampshire, in the summer of 1938 for Lincoln Kirstein's Ballet Caravan. The scenario, devised by Kirstein, concerns the brief life of William Bonney (1859–1881) who, like Copland, was born in Brooklyn.
Copland summarises the story:

The action begins and closes on the open prairie. The central portion of the ballet concerns itself with significant moments in the life of Billy the Kid. The first scene is a street in a frontier town. Familiar figures amble by. Cowboys saunter into town, some on horseback, others with their lassoes. Some Mexican women do a Jarabe which is interrupted by a fight between two drunks. Attracted by a gathering crowd, Billy is seen for the first time as a boy of twelve with his mother. The brawl turns ugly, guns are drawn and, in some unaccountable way, Billy's mother is killed. Without an instant's hesitation, in cold fury, Billy draws a knife from a cowhand's sheath and stabs his mother's slayers. His short but famous career had begun. In swift succession, we see episodes in Billy's later life. At night, under the stars in a quiet card game with his outlaw friends. Hunted by a posse led by his former friend Pat Garrett. Billy is pursued. A running gun battle ensues. Billy is captured. A drunken celebration takes place. Billy in prison is, of course, followed by one of Billy's legendary escapes. Tired and worn in the desert, Billy rests with his girl. (Pas de deux). Starting from a deep sleep, he senses movement in the shadows. The posse has finally caught up with him. It is the end.[5]

The ballet opens with an evocation of the loneliness of the prairie. The stark fifths of the harmony emphasise the emptiness of the scene. The change to the frontier-town street is marked by a perky theme on a piccolo (Ex. 48), to

Ex. 48

be played in the stage performance by a tin whistle. This tune is derived from the first of the cowboy tunes Copland uses, called 'Great Granddad'. Two other cowboy songs are alluded to: 'The Streets of Laredo' and 'The Old Chisholm

[5] 'Notes on a Cowboy Ballet' reprinted in Ballet Suite score, Boosey and Hawkes, 1941.

Trail'. As in *El Salón México*, Copland does not quote the
tunes in their original versions but in his own adaptations
(Ex. 49(a) and (b)). Against the duple time of the songs,

Ex. 49

Copland introduces fragments of waltz rhythms to suggest
the drunken state of the characters on stage. Two
trombones refer briefly to 'Git Along Little Dogies'. The
Mexican dance with its use principally of $\frac{5}{8}$ rhythms is based
on the cowboy song 'Come Wrangle yer Bronco', transfor-
med into a more exotic form (Ex. 50). The last tune
incorporated into this scene is 'Goodbye Old Paint', which
appears almost complete on oboe and violins (Ex. 51) after
several earlier hints.

Ex. 50

Ex. 51

'Prairie Night (Card Game at Night)' is an interlude
creating an atmosphere of calm before the following 'Gun
Battle'. It is loosely based on 'Oh Bury Me Not on the Lone
Prairie', a sentiment appropriate for Billy in his
predicament. The gunfire of the ensuing 'Gun Battle' is
vividly portrayed by muted trumpets and side drum.

There is an element of sardonic humour in the 'Celebration' of the townsfolk rejoicing at the capture of the outlaw. This is effected by giving the C major tune a bass line a semitone higher, in C sharp (Ex. 52). Perhaps we are expected to feel support for the anti-hero, now in the hands of a hostile mob. The deliberate crudity of the music confines the rejoicing to those on stage without arousing the same response in the audience.

Ex. 52

The orchestral suite omits the music of Billy's escape and the love *pas de deux* with his Mexican girlfriend in the desert. This includes a further variant of the tune 'Come Wrangle yer Bronco'.

The ballet ends with Billy's death and a return to the open prairie. The triumphant end suggests that our sympathies lie with the outlaw, despite his crimes, not with his enemies and the rule of law.

In this ballet Copland is wholly American. The legendary story and the treatment of cowboy songs produced his first totally 'national' work. Its considerable success confirmed for him that the deliberate change in direction, away from abstract music, was bringing his music to appreciative audiences. With choreography by Eugene Loring and decor by Jared French, it was first performed on two pianos, the pianists being Arthur Gold and Walter Hendl. On 26 May 1939 the ballet was revived at the Martin Beck Theatre, New York, by Ballet Theatre with the orchestral version conducted by Fritz Kitzlinger. In 1940 the composer produced from the score a concert suite in seven movements comprising about two-thirds of the original.

An Outdoor Overture
Following the success of *The Second Hurricane*, Copland wrote

An Outdoor Overture for the orchestra of the High School of Music and Art in New York. It was premiered there on 10 December 1938, conducted by Alexander Richter. In 1941 the composer made an arrangement for concert band. As he explained in a programme note: 'When Mr Richter first heard me play it from the piano sketch, he pointed out that it had an open-air quality. Together we hit upon the title'. This lively extravert work recaptures the exuberance of the school opera completed a year earlier.

Lark

From 1938 to 1940 Copland devoted himself to shorter works, and especially music for the stage and screen. The short choral item, *Lark*, a setting of a poem by the American poetess Genevieve Taggard (1894–1948), is scored for baritone solo and mixed voices.

The Five Kings

For Orson Welles' production *The Five Kings*, based on several Shakespeare plays, Copland composed incidental music comprising brief interludes and cue music scored for five instruments. The performance was first staged at the Mercury Theatre in Boston on 27 February 1939. The music remains unpublished.

Quiet City

At the request of Harold Clurman, Copland next provided music for *Quiet City*, an experimental play by Irwin Shaw (b. 1913) dealing with the night thoughts of different city dwellers. In *The Fervent Years* Clurman, who produced the play, provides an insight into the problems presented by *Quiet City*:[6]

> The play, a mixture of realism and fantasy in unsteady relation, was replete with pages of fine writing and eloquent dramatic scenes. Its theme, the recurrent one of the troubled conscience of the middle class that cannot quite reconcile

[6] p. 247.

itself to its life in a distraught world – which, when it retains
its honesty and sensitivity, it identifies with a life of sin – was
here given full orchestration. Because of the unevenness of
style, however, it was extraordinarily difficult to produce
satisfactorily. It needed a very free treatment, while we were
unable to give it anything but a skeletal production squeezed
on to the stage of the Belasco which still housed the massive
'Gentle People' (Irwin Shaw) sets. We had not been able to
raise money for the play – it was too experimental – and
produced it with our own funds. We presented the play on
two Sunday evenings to an audience as unconvinced as the
company was sure. We decided not to subject the production
to further public scrutiny. All that remained of our hard
work was a lovely score by Aaron Copland, which is not
infrequently heard nowadays at orchestral concerts.

The original scoring was for clarinet, saxophone, trumpet
and piano. Although the play did not survive its initial
production by the Group Theatre, New York, on 16 April
1939, the composer adapted the music in the following year,
arranging the score for cor anglais, trumpet and strings. In
this version, first presented by Daniel Saidenberg and his
Little Symphony Orchestra in New York on 28 January
1941, it has become one of his best-loved short works, is
frequently heard in concerts and has been recorded several
times.

From Sorcery to Science

For the New York World's Fair in May 1939, Copland was
commissioned to provide music for a marionette play, *From
Sorcery to Science*, presented in the Hall of Pharmacy. The
music for an orchestra of 35 players was recorded and
played on discs at each performance. As with *The Five Kings*,
the music remains unpublished.

The City

Also for the World's Fair in May 1939, Copland composed his
first film score for a documentary, *The City*, produced by
Pare Lorenz. The music was conducted by Max Goberman,
and two excerpts, 'New England Countryside' and 'Sunday
Traffic', were later used in *Music for Movies* of 1942.

Of Mice and Men

In Hollywood in October 1939 Copland composed the music for the Hal Roach film of John Steinbeck's *Of Mice and Men*. The premiere took place at the Roxy Theatre, New York, on 16 February 1940. Two excerpts, 'Barley Wagons' and 'Threshing Machines' were incorporated into *Music for Movies*.

John Henry

In 1939 the Columbia Broadcasting System commissioned a number of composers to write short pieces based on American folk-songs. Copland chose *John Henry*, which he scored for chamber orchestra. It was performed by Howard Barlow and the Columbia Broadcasting Symphony Orchestra on 5 March 1940, and subsequently has been taken into the repertoire of numerous amateur orchestras. It was revised in 1952 and performed in this version at the National Music Camp at Interlochen, Michigan, in the following year.

Our Town

Returning to Hollywood in March 1940, Copland began work on the music for the United Artists film version of Thornton Wilder's play *Our Town*, produced by Sol Lesser. Again the score was performed by Howard Barlow and the Columbia Broadcasting Symphony Orchestra. The concert version, consisting of a single movement, in a sustained tranquil mood, and lasting nine minutes, was performed on 9 June 1940, four days prior to the film premiere in Radio City Music Hall, New York. In 1944 Copland arranged three excerpts for piano and included another ('Grovers Corners') in *Music for Movies*.

In the summer of 1940 began his long association with the Boston Symphony's Tanglewood Summer School, where he taught composition for the next twenty-five years. Tanglewood (near Lenox, Massachusetts) is the summer home of the Boston Symphony Orchestra. Since 1937 the Berkshire Music Festival there has sponsored a summer school of music attended by performers and composers.

Distinguished musicians from America and Europe act as artists-in-residence, holding master-classes and presenting concerts.

Episode

In 1940 Copland contributed a short work for organ entitled *Episode* to a collection of pieces by American composers published by the H. Gray Music Publishing Company. (The other contributors included Frederick Jacobi, Douglas Moore, Walter Piston, Roger Sessions, Leo Sowerby and Bernard Wagenaar.) His only work to be written originally for organ (there is also a transcription of the *Preamble for a Solemn Occasion*), it begins with a gradual crescendo that leads to a quiet rumination on the interval of a falling major third. The final page reverses the opening section to end with a single quiet note.

Piano Sonata

Ten years after the *Piano Variations*, Copland began his Piano Sonata, which was completed in Chile in September 1941 while he was on an extended visit to Latin America. The

Copland giving a composition class at Tanglewood in the 1940s; Ned Rorem is second on the left (Photo by H.S. Babbitt Jr).

first sketches dated from 1935 but work was discontinued until 1939. It was the first full-length work since the _Short Symphony_ (1933) and _Statements_ (1934), and is dedicated to the playwright Clifford Odets (1906–1963), who had commissioned it. The composer gave the first performance at a concert of La Nueva Musica in Buenos Aires on 21 October 1941. A contemporary description of Copland as a performer was given by Samuel Lipman, the pianist and critic:[7]

> His playing on the piano of predominantly glassy sonority has given pianists a clear aural image of what he as a composer desires; his technical facility and rhythmic snap have been of great help in establishing the style in which his pieces are performed.

Like the _Piano Variations_, the Sonata is an intensely serious and personal work and was similarly received with only mute respect from the critics at the New York premiere on 9 January 1943. The performer was John Kirkpatrick.

The reversion to a musical language close to that of the _Piano Variations_ gives the impression that in the midst of writing overtly popular music Copland had an artistic need to please himself with an abstract work of ascetic introversion. The fiercely dissonant harmonies which predominate are quite uncompromising.

The extended improvisatory character of the outer movements does not possess the tight economy and single-minded unity of the _Variations_, and the Sonata, furthermore, is cast in a slow-fast-slow design. The first movement in B flat minor has a basically classical sonata form. It opens with two motto themes (Ex 53(a) and (b)), a descending triad, polytonally harmonised, and five-note phrases closely related to the theme of the _Piano Variations_. Notable at the outset are Copland's characteristic closely packed chords, especially low in the bass. His avoidance of conventional piano figuration leads one to imagine the music in orchestral terms, even more so than the _Piano Variations_. The

[7] In the sleeve note to the recording of the Sonata on New World Records (NW 277).

second subject in an alternating G major/minor is derived
from the descending thirds of the first bar. The *allegro*
section which ends the development recalls with its frequent changes of time signature another earlier work, the
Short Symphony.

Ex. 53

The second movement, marked *Vivace*, is a scherzo of
mercurial lightness, with hints of jazz (Ex. 54). As in the
previous movement, the second subject (Trio) is derived
from the opening bars, answered by the sequence of sixths
taken from the accompanying left hand (Ex. 55).

Ex. 54

Ex. 55

The finale, *Andante sostenuto*, like the first movement, opens with three chords (Ex. 56), basically in G major. Wilfrid Mellers observed:

> It is not an accident that these two movements of frustrated energy should lead – by way of a strange reminiscence of the first movement, all telescoped tonics and dominants, like a sublimated hill-billy stomp – into an Andante which is a quintessential expression of immobility.[8]

Ex. 56

Here also the writing implies orchestral instruments. A passage of simple canon can be heard as a conversation between, say, clarinet and bassoon. Copland recalls music from both the trio of the second movement and the opening of the first movement. The final bars (Ex. 57) are clearly derived from the descending triad of the beginning of the Sonata.

Ex. 57

[8] *op. cit.*, p. 92.

Not until the *Piano Fantasy*, completed in 1957, was Copland to return to this private musical world. For the remainder of the decade he was content to provide the musical public with pieces that presented few difficulties to the listener.

Las Agachadas

In 1942 the New York Schola Cantorum commissioned several composers to provide settings of folk songs from *Folk Songs and Poetry of Spain and Portugal*, compiled by Kurt Schindler, the founder of the Schola Cantorum. In a note on the title page of the score Hugh Ross, its first conductor, explained:

> 'Las Agachadas' is a dance-song, and Copland has realised the underlying spirit of the dance in the most original way, by treating the main chorus as a band which punctuates the verses with its thrumming refrain. The main melody is given to a small group who must sing with robust and unpolished freedom in peasant style.

This attractive setting in Spanish with an English translation is well within the capability of a school choir.

Lincoln Portrait

Lincoln Portrait was commissioned by André Kostelanetz, to whom the work is dedicated. It was intended that the music should reflect aspects of American life, exemplifying characteristics of the national spirit – courage, dignity, strength, simplicity and humour. The work is written for narrator and full orchestra, although the speaker does not enter until over half-way through the piece. The choice of texts is taken from Abraham Lincoln's speeches and letters, including the famous 'the government of the people, by the people, for the people shall not perish from the earth'. The words themselves are impressive but an element of the ludicrous and banal is introduced when the narrator separates each quotation by short 'biographical details': 'When standing erect he was six feet four inches tall: and this is what he said. He said. . .'. In spite of Copland's injunction at the head of the score that 'The speaker is

Copland by candlelight – a rather romantic view of the composer at work, in a photograph by Victor Kraft.

cautioned against undue emphasis in the delivery of Lincoln's words', it is hardly possible to recite some of the narration with complete seriousness.

In a conversation with Phillip Ramey,[9] Copland explained his choice of subject:

> I wanted to do Walt Whitman, but Kostelanetz had asked three composers for portraits – Virgil Thomson, Jerome Kern and myself – and since Kern was doing another literary figure, Mark Twain, I was asked to choose a statesman. Well, I started thinking of statesmen. Washington? Couldn't imagine it – too stiff and formal. But Lincoln appealed very much to me, and so, in order to learn about him, I got Lord Charnwood's biography.[10] There I found quotations of Lincoln that I thought would make him come more alive for an audience and that gave me the idea of using a speaker.

As an anonymous record sleeve note indicates,[11] the *Lincoln Portrait* can be divided into three sections:

[9] Reproduced on the sleeve of the CBS recording 72872.
[10] *Abraham Lincoln*, Constable, London, 1916.
[11] Columbia ML 5347.

The first suggests something of the mystery and sense of fatality that surrounds Lincoln's personality as well as the President's gentleness and simplicity of spirit. The middle section sketches briefly the lively times in which Lincoln lived. In the last section, says the composer, he attempts to draw a simple but impressive frame about the words of Lincoln himself.

The first section contains two subjects in a sonata-form exposition. It opens with a dotted figure that recalls the tempo and character of the second *Statement*. By the eighth bar it has become a melodic phrase (Ex. 58) which is used

Ex. 58

extensively in the first and third sections. In customary Copland fashion, the possibilities of this simple phrase are at once revealed. The violins and violas present the theme in fanfare manner, with widened intervals but still clearly recognisable (Ex. 59). In contrast to the dotted rhythms of

Ex. 59

the music to this point, the second subject is a simple *legato* melody, a version of the American folk-song 'Springfield Mountain', transformed from a fast, lively comic song to a slow expressive melody (Ex. 60). An altered version of Ex.

Ex. 60

60 on the trumpet recalls the *cantabile* trumpet solo which closes the final *Statement* ('Prophetic'). Before this theme can

be developed, the second section of the work bursts in with
the full orchestra let loose in an *allegro*. It is the music which
presents an aural impression of American life. The use of
sleigh bells suggests a horse and carriage speeding along a
19th-century New England country road. The fragment of
melody heard on the oboe (Ex. 61) is almost certainly a

Ex. 61

folk-song, although as yet unidentified. What seems to be a
derivative of this theme is a quotation from 'The Camptown
Races' by Stephen Foster, although only a few bars of the
chorus are recognisable. As the music calms down towards
the entry of the speaker, Copland re-introduces the
'Springfield Mountain' theme as a noble chorale in canon.
The four-note phrases separate the sentences of the text, so
that the narrator speaks while the instruments are resting
on longer notes. The dotted figure of the opening bars
returns as an accompanying figure to the speaker; the
starkness of the beginning of the work re-appears, as a
sonata-form recapitulation, although, as always with
Copland, this is no mere repetition, but a different presentation of the original material.

Again like the last *Statement*, Copland closes the work with
a simple *cantabile* trumpet melody. After the final words of
the speaker, the orchestra breaks into a monumental coda
that blazes out *fff*, resembling the ending of another earlier
work, the *Symphonic Ode*.

I. American Consciousness: ii
(1942–1945)

By 1942, the United States had been drawn into the Second World War. The disaster of Pearl Harbor on 7 December 1941, followed less than a month later by Hitler's declaration of war on America brought about an immediate heightening of national consciousness. *Lincoln Portrait* and *Fanfare for the Comman Man* (see above, pp. 87–90, and below, pp. 103–111) were part of Copland's response to the surge of patriotic fervour, and further established him as a major musical voice of the nation.

Rodeo

The considerable success of *Billy the Kid* encouraged the Ballet Russe de Monte Carlo to commission a second 'cowboy' ballet. With choreography by Agnes de Mille, who danced in it, *Rodeo* or 'The Courting at Burnt Ranch' captures the flavour of the American Western. Copland composed the music in Stockbridge, Massachusetts, between May and September 1942. The first performance was given by the Ballet Russe de Monte Carlo in the Metropolitan Opera House, New York, on 16 October, conducted by Franz Allers, with settings by Oliver Smith and costumes by Kermit Love. From the score the composer extracted *Four Dance Episodes* first heard complete under Alexander Smallens at the Lewisohn Stadium with the New York Philharmonic Symphony Orchestra on 22 June 1943. Only five minutes of music from the ballet are omitted in the Episodes.

Rodeo tells the story of a young cowgirl who has always been a tomboy. With her sudden awareness of the opposite sex, she attempts to attract the attention of the Head Wrangler and the Champion Roper. Her prowess as a rider does not impress them, and when they ride off after ignoring her exhibition she is left behind in tears. A group of girls from the city in pretty dresses arrives at the invitation of the Rancher's daughter. They are an instant success with the men, much to the angry dismay of the cowgirl, still dressed in dungarees and riding boots. She rushes from the scene, to return in the middle of the Saturday Night Dance in a party dress. Her transformation brings all the men to her side and she triumphantly accepts the Roper as her partner.

The introduction to the first Episode, 'Buckeroo Holiday', uses syncopation and brittle orchestration more reminiscent of *El Salón México* than *Billy the Kid* (Ex. 62). But like *Billy the Kid*, *Rodeo* incorporates folk-songs not quoted literally but presented with Copland's personal treatment. The first, 'Sis Joe', is preceded by 23 bars of 'vamping'. The second folk-song, 'If he'd be a buckaroo by his trade', like 'Sis Joe', was taken from the collection of tunes, *Our Singing Country*, compiled by John A. and Alan Lomax. This, too, has a simple rag-time accompaniment, humorously punctuated by empty bars. The treatment of the material also recalls the 'Jingo' movement of *Statements* with a brusque, almost satirical, character that serves to poke masculine fun at the pathetic figure of the cowgirl.

Ex. 62

The contrasting sadness of 'Corral Nocturne' serves to emphasise the isolation of the heroine in her rejection by the cowboys and her alienation from the city girls in their pretty dresses. Although the music contains no folk-song quotations, it evokes the mood of Copland's earlier pastoral episodes in *Music for Radio*, *Billy the Kid* and *Our Town*.

'Saturday Night Waltz' begins with the string instruments testing their open strings in the way a fiddler tunes up. The Waltz itself is in slow tempo, with hints of the song 'Goodbye old Paint', almost an echo from *Billy the Kid*.

The final episode, 'Hoe Down', is based on 'Bonyparte', a tune Copland found in *Traditional Music of American* by Ira

Ford, although, despite its American pedigree, it must have an origin in the Old World. A brief quote of 'McLeod's Reel' (Ex. 63) further emphasises a Scottish connection, although the jazzy treatment makes the whole movement distinctly American.

Ex. 63

In his autobiography Darius Milhaud wrote:

> What strikes one immediately in Copland's work is the feeling of the soul of his own country: the wide plains with their soft colourings, where the cowboy sings his nostalgic songs in which, even when the violin throbs and leaps to keep up with the pounding dance rhythms, there is always a tremendous sadness, an underlying distress, which nevertheless does not prevent them from conveying the sense of sturdy strength and sun-drenched movement. His ballet *Rodeo* gives perfect expression to this truly national art.[1]

Its popularity with audiences (and orchestras) is attributable to the direct appeal of melodic and rhythmic invention. George Amberg commented:

> Aaron Copland's score has body and richness and it is just as genuine and honest and just as unselfconscious in its use of American source material as the choreography.[2]

Music for Movies
In 1942 Copland extracted for a suite entitled *Music for Movies* five episodes from the film scores composed a few years earlier: *The City* (1939), *Our Town* (1940), and *Of Mice and Men* (1939). The individual movements possess

[1] *Notes Without Music*, Dobson, London, 1949, p. 253.
[2] *Ballet in America*, Duell, Sloan and Pearce, New York, 1949, p. 56.

With Darius Milhaud at Tanglewood, photographed by Victor Kraft in the 1950s.

sufficient descriptive character to survive effectively even when divorced from their visual associations. The five movements are:

    I. New England Countryside (*The City*),
   II. Barley Wagons (*Of Mice and Men*),
  III. Sunday Traffic (*The City*),
  IV. Story of Grovers Corners (*Our Town*),
   V. Threshing Machines (*Of Mice and Men*).

Although the first performance was given in New York in 1943, for some unaccountable reason the score was not published until 1970. Perhaps not one of the composer's major works, it is accessible music for student orchestras which might be daunted by his technically more complex orchestral compositions.

Danzón Cubano

In 1941 Copland visited Cuba as part of a goodwill tour of nine Latin-American countries, sponsored by the United States Committee for the Co-ordination of Inter-American Relations. *Danzón Cubano* was composed in Oakland, New Jersey, at the end of 1942 to celebrate the 20th anniversary of the League of Composers and first performed in the version for two pianos by the composer and Leonard Bernstein in the Town Hall, New York, on 9 December 1942.

> The danzón is a well-known dance form in Cuba and other Latin-American countries. It is not a fast dance, however, and should not be confused with the rhumba, conga or samba. It fulfils a function rather similar to the waltz in our dance, providing contrast for the more animated numbers. Usually constructed in two parts which are thematically independent, the special charm of the danzón is a certain naive sophistication, alternating in mood between passages of rhythmic precision and a kind of non-sentimental sweetness.[3]

To the normal full symphony orchestra and now-customary piano, Copland adds Latin-American percussion instruments – claves, maracas and gourd, and an item not usual in a symphony orchestra, a cow bell.

Unlike *El Salón México*, *Danzón Cubano* is derived from melodic and rhythmic fragments noted by the composer during several visits to Cuba. Copland states that in no sense is it intended to be an authentic *danzón*, but an American tourist's impression of a Cuban dance form. The orchestral transcription of 1945 makes the work a companion 'travel souvenir' to *El Salón México*.

Copland incorporates four distinct themes into an adapted rondo form, with the opening motto recurring several times although all the themes re-appear after their initial presentation (Ex. 64). In spite of frequent changes of time-signature to accommodate the different rhythmic figures, a basic constant tempo is maintained throughout,

---

[3] Uncredited note in full score, Boosey and Hawkes, 1949.

since this is a single *danzón*, not a sequence of dances. While some of the syncopations are derived from Cuban rhythms, most irregular note-patterns and misplaced accents are symptomatic of Copland's style.

Ex. 64

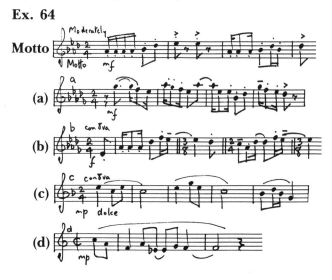

Fanfare for the Common Man

For performance during the 1942–43 season of the Cincinnati Symphony Orchestra, Eugene Goossens commissioned ten American composers to write patriotic fanfares. The composers chosen included Henry Cowell, Paul Creston, Howard Hanson, Walter Piston, Deems Taylor, Virgil Thomson and Bernard Wagenaar. Copland composed his *Fanfare for the Common Man* for brass and percussion. He later used it as the introduction to the finale of the Third Symphony, and in this context it will be discussed in more detail below (pp. 103–111).

North Star

In February 1943 Copland again went to Hollywood to work on the score for the RKO film *North Star*, based on a story by Lillian Hellman, produced by Samuel Goldwyn and directed by Lewis Milestone. As the film was set in Russia, he deliberately adopted certain Russian characteristics especially in a chorus entitled 'Song of the Fatherland'. From the music he produced two published items *The Song of the Guerrillas* for baritone, male chorus, and piano (or organ) and *The Younger Generation* for treble voices (SSA), or mixed chorus and piano (arranged by Frederic Fay Swift). The words of both are by Ira Gershwin.

Violin Sonata

The Sonata for Violin and Piano, begun in 1942 in Oakland, New Jersey, and completed the following year in Hollywood, differs in character from the *Piano Variations* and Piano Sonata in that it adopts a simpler style with a strong relationship to folk-music, although all the melodic material is original. Much of the music is in a hymn-like, pastoral vein, elegiac in mood and sparse in texture. Julia Smith suggests[1] that the composition of the ballet *Appalachian Spring*, written at the same time, had an effect upon the Violin Sonata. It is dedicated to the memory of Lieutenant Harry H. Dunham, a close friend of Copland's who died in action in the South Pacific in 1943.

The first movement, in sonata form, opens with a slow introduction which presents a five-note motto theme on the violin interpolated between block chords on the piano that suggest the solemn austerity of New England hymnody (Ex. 65). In characteristic manner, Copland builds the entire movement on this simple motto figure, which evolves into

Ex. 65

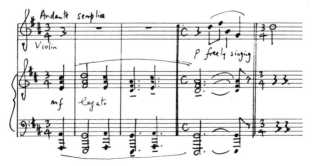

[1] *op. cit.*, p. 235.

the principal theme of the movement. The implied G major tonality at the outset is now confirmed (Ex. 66). The

Ex. 66

simultaneous use of tonic and dominant harmonies in the piano in the opening bars is developed when Copland introduces the second subject on the violin in D major against the piano's insistent repetition of the first theme, still basically in G major. The character of the movement alternates between contrapuntal, mainly canonical exploitation of the material and a lyrical flow of slower melody on the violin, punctuated by cadential phrases on the piano. These perfect cadences have the effect of an 'Amen' at the end of each phrase. The recapitulation (beginning in C major), marked 'with repose', brings back both themes: the movement closes in G major with a varied repetition of the music of the introduction.

The second movement, *Lento*, is in ABA form. Here the plainness of texture, so fundamental to the whole work, reaches its extreme. A simple melody of rising and falling pentatonic scales on the piano provides a gently undulating accompaniment for the *cantus-firmus*-like modal theme of the violin. The tonality is D major with a flattened leading note. A bridge passage of four bars recalls the motto of the previous movement. The second subject is built on descending triads of E minor and G major against a rocking alternation of two chords on the piano. The reversion to the first theme is again made by way of the five-note motto on the piano. The D major of the close prepares for the G major of the Finale which follows without a break. In this movement also, the flattened leading note gives a modal effect. The form of this *allegro* is a modified rondo: A–B–C–A–B–C–A–C–coda.

The principal theme on unaccompanied violin (Ex. 67) has the character of a fugue subject and is later treated

Ex. 67

canonically with the piano, but it is not a fugue. After the scurrying semi-quavers, the second subject (Ex. 68),

Ex. 68

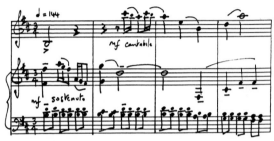

although related to the foregoing, is more lyrical. The third theme is derived from the rising figure at the beginning of the first subject. All three passages return in the same order but with a new working of the material. Following the exhilarating climax, the headlong impetus of the movement dissolves into a slower tempo, to prepare for the coda, based on the music of the opening of the Sonata. The motto figure, reduced to its first four notes, concludes the work in an elegiac vein.

The Violin Sonata is Copland's most accessible and appealing instrumental piece. The economical use of melodic and harmonic resources is wholly characteristic of the composer, and in a manner that allows the listener to feel a relationship between the three movements.

Appalachian Spring

While in Hollywood working on the music for *North Star*, Copland received a commission from the Elizabeth Sprague Coolidge Foundation to write a ballet for Martha Graham. The first sketches were made in June 1943 and the score completed in the following year in Cambridge, Massachusetts, where he was teaching at Harvard University.

The ballet *Appalachian Spring*, with its original scoring for 13 instruments, was first produced in the Coolidge Auditorium of the Library of Congress in Washington on 30 October 1944. Not until the day before the first performance was the title *Appalachian Spring*, taken from a poem by Hart Crane, given to the work. On that occasion it shared a triple bill with Milhaud's *Jeux de Printemps* (Martha Graham's title was *Imagined Wing*) and Hindemith's *Hérodiade*. Martha Graham danced the principal role with Merce Cunningham, Eric Hawkins and May O'Donnell. The conductor was Louis Horst. It received the New York Music Critics' Circle Award for the outstanding theatrical work of the 1944–45 season and won the Pulitzer Prize for music in 1945.

The story, set in the early 19th century, tells of the preparations for a wedding in a Pennsylvania farming community. Although the music reflects the folk-songs of the Appalachians, the only quotation is the Shaker song 'Simple Gifts' on which the composer writes a sequence of variations.

The original score, lasting about eight minutes longer than the 26 minutes of the concert suite, is in one continuous act, falling into linked sections.

I. The slow, quiet opening introduces the principal characters, the bride and bridegroom, the preacher, and a neighbour.

II. *Allegro*. A lively dance, in A major, recalls fiddle music, with typical Copland cross-rhythms (Ex. 69).

Ex. 69

Against this, the composer introduces a four-note motto in longer notation derived from the introduction. This provides a melodic link with the following section.

III. *Moderato*. A slower dance for the bride and groom of affecting tender simplicity.

    IV. Fast. The preacher and his congregation join the couple in a barn-dance.

    V. Solo for the bride; this joyful dance is derived from the music of Section II.

    VI. Return of the music of the introduction.

    VII. The Shaker melody, 'Simple Gifts', appears first in the clarinet (Ex. 70) and is followed by four variations.

Ex. 70

    VIII. Before the final statement of the tune on the full orchestra, as in the concert suite, there is an extended passage, mostly comprising new material, but making some passing references back to ideas in Sections I, III, and IV, ending with a brief reappearance of the Shaker melody before its full concluding version.

    IX. The material of the introduction forms the basis of the close of the ballet to portray the newly married couple left alone on the steps as the guests depart. With quiet confidence and hope for the future they enter their home.

This appealing score marks Copland's most traditional standpoint in his progress away from the austerity and dissonance of the works at the beginning of his composing career. Although only one genuine folk-song appears in the ballet, it must be seen as the epitome of his 'American' style. Even divorced from the visual aspects on stage, every bar of *Appalachian Spring* has its roots in the countryside of New England, and will long remain a strong expression of national feeling.

Letter from Home

In 1943 Paul Whiteman and the American Broadcasting

Companies (ABC) commissioned works from several American composers. Copland's contribution, *Letter from Home*, was written at Harvard University and Tepoztlan, Mexico, during 1944. It was first played on the Philco Radio Show on 17 October 1944. As the original version was scored for the special instrumentation of a radio orchestra, Copland made a shorter version of it for the normal small orchestra. This score was published in 1962. Although one of the composer's slighter works, it possesses a lyrical charm in its pastoral melodic invention. Belonging in character to the music for the theatre and film, it is a more substantial score than *John Henry* or *Our Town* and like those pieces is a fitting repertoire item for college and amateur orchestras.

Jubilee Variation
In 1945, as he had done three years earlier, Eugene Goossens asked ten composers to write short pieces, this time for the Golden Jubilee of the Cincinnati Orchestra. Each composer contributed a variation on a theme provided by Goossens. Copland's *Jubilee Variation* was performed in March 1945, but its brevity – it lasts a mere three minutes – has caused the piece to remain unpublished.

The Cummington Story
For the Overseas Unit of the United States Office of War Information in January 1945, Copland composed a score for a documentary film *The Cummington Story*.

VI. The Third Symphony

(1944–1946)

After the completion of *Appalachian Spring* in 1944 Copland began work on his most extended orchestral composition, the Third Symphony. In the previous year he had received a commission from the Koussevitzky Music Foundation, and in July 1944, in Tepoztlan, he began the initial sketches. He continued on the Symphony in several different locations from October 1944 to September 1946: New York; Bernardsville, New Jersey; New York; Ridgefield, Connecticut; New York; the MacDowell Colony, Peterborough, New Hampshire; Tanglewood, Massachusetts; and Richmond, Massachusetts. The final bars were completed on 29 September, less than a month before the premiere in Boston under Koussevitzky. The haste in finishing the score is indicated by the revision of the closing pages, where two short sections were omitted in later performances. Dedicated 'to the memory of my dear friend Natalie Koussevitzky', the Third Symphony gained the New York Music Critics' Circle Award for the best orchestral work of the 1946–47 concert season.

Inevitably the excursion into folk music for some of his recent compositions, especially the three ballets, left traces of a new style on the Symphony in spite of Copland's own remark that 'It contains no folk or popular material. Any reference to jazz or folk material in this work is purely unconscious'.[1] There is clearly no direct quotation of folksong, but the idiom of folk-song and dance is often present in all four movements.

In Copland's programme notes for the premiere he wrote of the first movement, *Molto moderato*:

> The opening movement, which is broad and expressive in character, opens and closes in the key of E major. (Formally it bears no relation to the sonata-allegro with which

---

[1] Programme note for the first performance.

symphonies usually begin.) The themes, three in number, are plainly stated: the first is on the strings at the very start without introduction; the second in related mood in violas and oboes; the third, of a bolder nature, in the trombones and horns. The general form is that of an arch, in which the central portion is more animated; and the final section is an extended coda, presenting a broadened version of the opening material. Both the first and third themes are referred to again in later movements of the Symphony.

Like those of so many American symphonies, the first movement acts as an introduction and is not a weighty sonata-form movement in the classical mould. The finale is the musical kernel of the work.

The opening of the Symphony (Ex. 71) resembles the beginning of *Appalachian Spring*, in Copland's customary self-effacing manner of embarking on a large-scale work,

Ex. 71

with simple melodic material quietly ushered in. The continuous unfolding of melody in crotchet note-values gives rise to the second subject (Ex. 72), basically the same in character as the first, but with a different outline.

Ex. 72

A feature of the first three pages of the score common to several earlier works, most notably the *Short Symphony*, is that much of the music is in unison, with brief passages of chordal counterpoint and two-part writing between the strings and brass. After an intricate development of both themes, the movement gathers momentum with a gradual increase of tempo. Although the music is clearly diatonic, the tonal bass is constantly modulating from bar to bar. The third theme (Ex. 73) is related to the preceding music, but more determined in character. As this theme is itself

Ex. 73

modulating, each repetition moves the music into new keys; thus in the canonical passage that follows, consecutive bars are unequivocally in the keys of C minor, B flat major, A flat major, G major, F major, and so on. The first three notes of this theme are later compressed into a figure (Ex. 74) which

Ex. 74

serves as the germ for the first subject of the following movement and plays a prominent part in the Fanfare which precedes the Finale. As with all Copland's extended symphonic movements, there is no simple recapitulation of the opening, but a reworking of earlier material to form the conclusion.

Of the Scherzo, Copland writes:

Allegro molto: the form of this movement stays closer to the normal symphonic procedure. It is the usual scherzo, with first part, trio and return. A brass introduction leads to the main theme, which is stated three times in Part 1: at first on horns and violas with continuation in clarinets, then in unison strings, and finally in augmentation in the lower brass. The three statements of the theme are separated by the usual episodes. After the climax is reached, the trio follows without a pause. Solo woodwinds sing the new trio melody in lyrical and canonical style. The recapitulation of Part 1 is not literal. The principal theme of the scherzo returns in a somewhat disguised form in the solo piano, leading through previous episodic material to a full restatement in the *tutti* orchestra. This is climaxed by a return to the lyrical trio, this time sung in canon and in *fortissimo* by the entire orchestra.

The Scherzo opens with a fanfare-like introduction of twenty-two bars, initiated by the horns and continued for the most part by the brass (Ex. 75). Before the theme itself

Ex. 75

is heard for the first time (on horns and violins), the fanfare is followed by nine bars of a new idea (Ex. 76) which is used later for the episodes. Copland's observance of the customary scherzo form in this movement even extends to maintaining F major as the key for each statement of the theme.

Ex. 76

The Trio is in complete contrast to the high spirits of the Scherzo. The lyrical oboe solo (Ex. 77), over sustained notes on clarinets, is further evidence of Copland's folk idiom in this work. The theme itself is not a folk-song but would not be out of place in the middle of *Rodeo* or *Appalachian Spring*,

Ex. 77

for it has all the qualities associated with American folk-song. A new section adding to this theme continues the lyrical mood of the Trio (Ex. 78), until the gradual return to the Scherzo begins with the 'disguised form' of the theme on the piano, and the movement ends with a massive statement of the opening fanfare now scored for the full orchestra reinforced by a barrage of percussion.

Ex. 78

Of the slow movement, *Andante quasi allegretto,* Copland writes that it

> is freest of all in formal structure. Although it is built up sectionally, the various sections are intended to emerge one from the other in continuous flow, somewhat in the manner of a close-knit series of variations. The opening section, however, plays no role other than that of introducing the main body of the movement. High up in the unaccompanied first violins is heard a rhythmically transformed version of the third (trombone) theme of the first movement of the Symphony. It is briefly developed in contrapuntal style, and comes to a full close, once again in the key of E major.
>
> A new and more tonal theme is introduced in the solo flute. This is the melody that supplies thematic substance for the sectional metamorphoses that follow: at first with quiet singing nostalgia; then faster and heavier – almost dance-like; then more child-like and naive, and finally vigorous and forthright. Imperceptibly the whole movement drifts off into the higher regions of the strings, out of which floats the single line of the beginning, sung by a solo violin and piccolo, accompanied this time by harps and celeste. The third movement calls for no brass, with the exception of a single horn and trumpet.

The slow movement opens with the first violins in their high register, playing a transformed version of the trombone theme of the first movement. A contrapuntal development of this theme prepares the way for the principal subject, a simple tune for flute (Ex. 79) that seems at first more like an accompanying melody than a significant theme in its own right, which later provides the material for almost the entire movement. From this point the tempo becomes progressively faster; this central section brings to mind the lively dances of *Appalachian Spring*. A new rhythmic and

Ex. 79

melodic figure inspired by the onward drive of the music appears first on the trumpet. In characteristic manner, Copland extends and adapts this theme. At the climax the principal subject is treated in close canon with one of the few passages of polytonality, so often seen in earlier works but seldom apparent in the Third Symphony. Other typical features of the composer's style evident here are the parallel movement of parts in sevenths and the rhythms of the melodic lines which fail to coincide with bar-lines. The movement ends almost exactly as it began with the high melody now on a solo violin playing harmonics against a quiet sustained chord.

Copland describes the last movement, *Allegro deliberato* (Fanfare) – *Allegro risoluto*, as follows:

> The final movement follows without a pause. It is the largest movement of the Symphony, and closest in structure to the customary sonata-allegro form. The opening fanfare is based on *Fanfare for the Common Man*, which I composed in 1942 at the invitation of Eugene Goossens for a series of wartime fanfares introduced under his direction by the Cincinnati Symphony. In the present version it is played first pianissimo by flutes and clarinets, and then suddenly given out by brass and percussion. The fanfare serves as a preparation for the movement which follows. The components of the usual form are there: a first theme in animated sixteenth-note [semiquaver] motion; a second theme – broader and more song-like in character; a full blown movement, leading to a peroration. One curious feature of the movement consists of the fact that the second theme is to be found embedded in the development section instead of being in its customary place. The development, as such, concerns itself with the fanfare and first theme fragments. A shrill 'tutti'

chord, with flutter-tongued brass and piccolos, brings the development to a close.

What follows is not a recapitulation in the ordinary sense. Instead a delicate interweaving of the first theme in the higher solo woodwinds is combined with a quiet version of the fanfare in the two bassoons.

Combined with this, the opening of the first movement is quoted, first in the violins, and later in the solo trombone. Near the end a full-voiced chanting of the second song-like theme is heard in horns and trombones. The Symphony concludes on a restatement of the opening phrase with which the entire work began.

The movement opens in the key of A flat with a *pianissimo* version of the fanfare on flutes and clarinets. At the entry of the fanfare (Ex. 80), itself at the eleventh bar, there is an

Ex. 80

abrupt change into C major. The fanfare, for brass and percussion, is then played in its complete 1942 version. Between the fanfare and the *allegro*, Copland inserts a five-bar transition passage (Ex. 81), in which lower strings,

Ex. 81

clarinet and bassoon quietly ruminate on the first phrases of
the fanfare. Over this a solo oboe hints at the *allegro* theme,
tentatively repeating the first note. In this way Copland
provides a compatible relationship, even at this early stage,
between two strongly contrasted elements, the fanfare and
the *allegro* theme. The hints on the oboe in the above extract
become the *allegro* theme itself as the music settles firmly
into D major (Ex. 82).

Ex. 82

The ensuing *fugato* as each of the woodwind wind takes up
derivatives of this figure is one of Copland's most delicate
and delightful creations. With the entry of strings and later
horns, the orchestra provides a highly charged impetus.
Considerable technical demands are made upon the players
– the violinists in particular have to possess light-fingered
virtuosity. At the climax (fig. 101) Copland brings back the
fanfare theme in woodwind and trumpets and in
augmentation on trombones, a piece of craftsmanship that
is a natural synthesis of musical material, and no mere
academic device.

A *pianissimo* statement of the fanfare combined with the
principal theme provide a background for the introduction
of the second theme, as Copland states, curiously
introduced at this late stage into the development. An
unusual feature of the new subject is the time-signature of
regular $\frac{3}{8} + \frac{2}{4}$ bars; this adds a new rhythmical interest, while
the violins continue their chatter of semiquavers.

The recapitulation, following a *fff* chord, is 'far from
literal', a characteristic of all his works in symphonic form,
but certain figures and treatments of themes already heard
make re-appearances sufficiently consistent to indicate that
the development has formally come to an end and the
recapitulation has begun, although now in D flat, a semitone
lower than the exposition.

In the coda, Copland combines the fanfare theme, at

times inverted, the opening theme of the first movement and both themes of the *allegro* of the finale. The majestic ending is an apotheosis of these thematic ideas now so consummately integrated. Of his earlier orchestral works only the *Symphonic Ode* in its concluding pages possesses a similar declamatory grandeur.

Darius Milhaud recognised[2] an emotional quality in the Third Symphony which might not be noticed by an American writer:

> His recent symphony has more grandeur and a deeper lyricism, but the melancholy simplicity of its themes are a direct expression of his own delicate sadness and sensitive heart.

VII. 'In the Beginning' 'The Red Pony' and The Clarinet Concerto

(1947—1949)

With the completion of the Third Symphony, the most ambitious of his orchestral compositions, Copland turned to music for mixed voices, a medium to which he had contributed only a handful of pieces.

In the Beginning
For the Harvard University 'Symposium on Music Criticism' in May 1947, Copland composed *In the Beginning*, his only extended choral work. Scored for mezzo-soprano (as narrator) and unaccompanied mixed chorus, it sets a text from the Book of Genesis, and is presented in rondo form with the refrain for each of the seven days of creation as the theme.

Much of the mezzo-soprano part is set as recitative, with the instruction by the composer that it should be sung 'in a gentle, narrative manner, like reading a familiar and oft-told story'. The music is continuous, with subtle changes of tempo within a basic pulse. Copland allows the natural inflexions of the words to provide flexible rhythms, often in passages of chanting, hymn-like chordal textures and at times without bar-lines. The directness of expression is emphasised by the syllabic setting of the words with vir-tually no melismata.

The variety of harmonic treatment, at times monodic, often in simple canon, with modal implications, and uncom-plicated polytonality, produces a timeless quality. Copland had composed only two other works for *a cappella* chorus, the *Four Motets* of 1921, not published until 1979, and *Lark* (1938). The medium allowed him to explore a new musical world in such a way that few characteristics of his other music are evident. Some fragments of melody (Ex. 83) provide echoes of orchestral works, especially of *Statements*

Ex. 83

and the Third Symphony. The jazzy rhythms and anti-phonal exchanges between the voices at times resemble orchestration, and the polytonal textures arise from the separate tonalities of the solo singer and the chorus (Ex. 84). In such instances the C flat/C natural combination provides a hint of negro 'blues'. It is a cause for regret that after the success of this minor masterpiece Copland explored the field of choral music no further.

Ex. 84

The Red Pony

The music for the film of John Steinbeck's *The Red Pony* was composed at the Republic Pictures Studio in the San Fernando Valley between February and April 1948; the producer-director, Lewis Milestone, had been responsible for the earlier Steinbeck film *Of Mice and Men* for which Copland had provided the score. The orchestral suite was created by the composer in response to a commission from

Efrem Kurtz for a work to open his first season with the Houston Symphony Orchestra.

In keeping with the story about a small boy and his pony, the musical language is simple, with echoes of folk-song. Although lacking the strikingly individual characteristics of the three 'Western' ballets, *The Red Pony* Suite has continued to earn popularity with its naïve charm. Virgil Thomson expressed a qualified appreciation for the original film score. He described it as 'the most elegant . . . yet composed and executed under "industry conditions", as Hollywood nowadays calls itself'.[1] The Suite was presented as a ballet by the Toledo (Ohio) Ballet Company on 24 February 1954.

In a programme note in the printed score Copland provided the following description of the suite:

> Steinbeck's well-known tale is a series of vignettes concerning a ten-year-old boy called Jody, and his life in a Californian ranch setting. There is a minimum of action of a dramatic or startling kind. The story gets its warmth and sensitive quality from the character studies of the boy, Jody, Jody's grandfather, the cow-hand Billy Buck, and Jody's parents, the Tiflins. The kind of emotions that Steinbeck evokes in his story are basically musical ones, since they deal so much with the unexpressed feelings of daily living. In shaping the suite I recast much of the musical material so that, although all the music may be heard in the film, it has been re-organized as to continuity for concert purposes.

The composer added that although some of the melodies in *The Red Pony* may sound rather folk-like, they were his own; there are no quotations of folk-song anywhere in the work.

The Suite is in six sections, as described by the composer in the Preface to the miniature score.

I. 'Morning on the Ranch':

> Sounds of daybreak. The daily chores begin. A folk-like melody suggests the atmosphere of simple country living.

---

[1] *The New York Herald-Tribune*, 10 April 1949; reprinted in *A Virgil Thomson Reader*, pp. 321–326.

The slow introduction on full orchestra gives way to a lively tune (Ex. 85), heard first on two flutes, later extended and taken up by the full orchestra.

Ex. 85

II. 'The Gift':

> Jody's father surprises him with the gift of a red pony. Jody shows off his new acquisition to his school chums, who cause quite a commotion about it. Jody was glad when they had gone. A slow quiet introduction based on brief melodic fragments gradually acquires momentum until a new dancing melody, like a folk-song, bursts in, depicting the boy's excitement when showing the pony to his school friends.

Ex. 86

This agitated movement breaks off suddenly, before a brief coda based on the opening bars.

III. (a) 'Dream March';
     (b) 'Circus Music':

> Jody has a way of going off into day-dreams. Two of them are pictured here. In the first, Jody imagines himself with Billy Buck at the head of an army of knights in silvery armour; in the second, he is a whip-cracking ringmaster at the circus.

The March is based on the principal theme of the previous movement, played polytonally in C major on a solo trumpet to an accompanying march-rhythm on the tuba in D.

'Circus Music' is appropriately scored for wind and percussion only.

IV. 'Walk to the Bunkhouse':
Billy Buck was a fine hand with horses and Jody's
admiration knew no bounds. This is a scene of two pals
on their walk to the bunkhouse.

Copland represents the shambling walk of the cowhand and
the boy with an irregular ostinato in the bass-line. Against
this he adds first a contrasting long note on the violins,
followed by a jaunty trumpet tune. The movement ends
with a combination of all three ideas (Ex. 87).

Ex. 87

V. 'Grandfather's Story':
Jody's grandfather retells the story of how he led a wagon
train clear across the plains to the coast. But he can't
hide his bitterness from the boy. Westerning has died out
of the people. Westerning isn't a hunger any more.

The movement begins sadly with a poignant cor anglais
melody (Ex. 88). As the grandfather recalls the hardship of
his youth, the music is transformed into an aggressive mood
of dissonance, later dispelled by the return of the sorrowful
opening.

Ex. 88

VI. 'Happy Ending':
Some of the title music is incorporated into the final
movement. There is a return to the folk-like melody of
the beginning, this time played with boldness and
conviction.

This movement is basically a repetition and a reworking of the material of the first movement to produce a triumphant close.

Four Piano Blues

Although published in 1949, the *Four Piano Blues* cover a wide span of the composer's career, the earliest dating from 1926. As the title suggests, these are slight pieces but nevertheless characteristic of the composer in relaxed mood.

No. 1, marked 'Freely poetic' and composed in 1947, is written in Copland's pastoral vein. It possesses an improvisatory quality with spare textures, and is contrapuntal in character. A repeated minor third is the predominant feature (Ex. 89). It is dedicated to Leo Smit.

Ex. 89

In No. 2, 'Soft and languid', the descending pattern of thirds in the right hand over two repeated chords in the bass (Ex. 90) provides the polytonal characteristic of a blues. The central section introduces a flowing melody which is later combined in the left hand with the return of the opening music. The second of the *Blues* dates from 1934, at a time when Copland was occupied with abstract works; it belongs in essence to the previous decade, and had originally appeared in the ballet *Hear Ye! Hear Ye!* In its new, revised form it is dedicated to Andor Foldes.

Ex. 90

No. 3, 'Muted and sensuous', is dedicated to William Kapell, the gifted American pianist who died in an air-crash in 1953 at the age of 31.[2] In compact rondo form, it contrasts a repeated chordal phrase with more lightly scored passages higher on the piano (Ex. 91).

Ex. 91

No. 4, 'With bounce', is dedicated to John Kirkpatrick, the American pianist active in the promotion of American music, especially of the works of Charles Ives, and who, like Copland, had studied with Nadia Boulanger in the 1920s.[3]

---

[2] In an obituary notice in *The New York Herald-Tribune* on 8 November 1953 (reprinted in *A Virgil Thomson Reader*, pp. 365–7), Virgil Thomson wrote:
Kapell had become a grown man and a mature artist, a master. He could play great music with authority; his readings of it were at once sound and individual. He had a piano technique of the first class, a powerful mind, a consecration and a working ability such as are granted to few, and the highest aspirations toward artistic achievement.

[3] Virgil Thomson, who has chronicled so much of this century's musical life in America and elsewhere, wrote (in *The New York Herald-Tribune* of 24 November 1943, reprinted in *A Virgil Thomson Reader*, pp. 243–4) that Kirkpatrick
has a way of making one feel happy about American music. He does this by loving it, understanding it, and playing it very beautifully. He plays, in fact, everything very beautifully that I have ever heard him play. But people who play that beautifully so rarely play American music that Mr Kirkpatrick's recitals are doubly welcome, once for their repertory and again for his unique understanding of it.
The loveliness of his playing comes from a combination of tonal delicacy with really firm rhythm. Exactitude with flexibility at all the levels of loudness is the characteristic of American pianism that transcends all our local schools of composition. It is what makes us a major musical people, and it is exactly this rhythmic quality that escapes our European interpreters. European tonal

Around Copland, photographed in Caracas in 1957, are eight composers, from the left, the Chilean Juan Orrego-Salas, the Spaniard Julian Orbon (who then lived in Cuba and now lives in New York), the Panamanian Roque Cordero, the Mexican Blas Galindo, the Cuban Harald Gramatges, the Uruguayan hector Tosar (represented by his drawing), the Puerto Rican Hector Campos Parsi, the Venezuelan Antonio Esteves, and best-known of all, the Argentinian Alberto Ginastera.

The fourth of the *Piano Blues* had been performed on its own by Hugo Balzo in Montevideo, Uruguay on 7 May 1942. It is the most overtly jazzy of the four, as one might expect from the date of composition, 1926. The cross-rhythms of the left hand and the vamping bass recall the Piano Concerto written at the same time.

The first public performance of all of the *Four Piano Blues* was given by Leo Smit at a League of Composers Concert in Carl Fischer Hall, New York on 13 March 1950, although the composer had recorded them for Decca in the previous year.

Clarinet Concerto

In 1948, to a commission from Benny Goodman, Copland completed the Concerto for clarinet, string orchestra, harp and piano. The first movement had been composed a year earlier in Rio de Janiero while Copland was on a goodwill tour of South America. Like the Piano Concerto, it is cast in two movements, the first slow and lyrical and linked by a virtuoso cadenza to the fast, jazzy finale. Premiered by

beauty, of course, more often than not escapes American pianists. Mr Kirkpatrick's combination of European tonal technique with full understanding of American rhythm makes his playing of American works a profoundly exciting thing and a new thing in music.

Goodman in November 1950, the Concerto was used in the following year for a ballet, *Pied Piper*, choreographed by Jerome Robbins for the New York City Ballet.

Copland provided the following analysis:

> The first movement is simple in structure, based upon the usual A–B–A song form. The general character of this movement is lyrical and expressive. The Cadenza that follows provides the soloist with considerable opportunities to demonstrate his prowess, at the same time introducing fragments of the melodic material to be heard in the second movement.
>
> Some of this material represents an unconscious fusion of elements obviously related to North and South American popular music. (For example, a phrase from a currently popular Brazilian tune, heard by the composer in Rio, became imbedded in the secondary material in F major.) The over-all form of the final movement is that of a free rondo, with several side issues developed at some length. It ends with a fairly elaborate coda in C major.

The special features of Benny Goodman's playing inevitably influenced much of the solo writing: the cool, lyrical quality of the first movement, the incisive rhythmical attack and 'hot' jazz of the cadenza, and in the second movement, the exploitation of the high register (including an optional double-top B flat), and the final glissando. All these features are characteristic of Goodman's style.

The first movement opens as a slow waltz with the simplest of accompaniments to the clarinet theme (Ex. 92).

Ex. 92

The second subject, similar in mood to the first, but with a different melodic outline, is also introduced by the clarinet after hints of it on the orchestra (Ex. 93). The cadenza is

Ex. 93

based on motifs which provide the principal material for the ensuing movement. Three figures in particular are predominant (Ex. 94). The tempo is gradually increased to

Ex. 94

prepare for the fast finale. The piano, which has remained silent in the first movement, now acquires an important role although, except for one brief solo of five bars, it is, like the harp, a member of the orchestra. Against an ostinato accompaniment, fragments of the rondo theme appear on the orchestra before the soloist offers it in a more complete form (Ex. 95). The episodes are built upon the ideas heard

Ex. 95

earlier in the cadenza. And the perky dancing rhythms are a reminder of the ballet scores, with a verve that sets one's foot tapping. Some passages introduce contrasting cross-rhythms, an echo of the *Short Symphony*.

The original soloist was given several opportunities for playing in his more customary jazz style (Ex. 96); and Copland makes considerable technical demands upon the orchestra as well as the soloist — the first violins in particular have passages where virtuosity is required.

Ex. 96

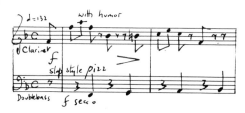

Commenting in 1955, Julia Smith was fulsome in her praise:[4]

As to whether the Clarinet Concerto is to be classed among the composer's great works, we are much too close in time to judge. However, in formulating even a temporary judgement of the work, we must again reflect on the composer's intentions. A commission for Benny Goodman (to perform himself) who is generally regarded as our most outstanding 'popular' clarinetist and one of our significant swing-band leaders whose strongest appeal is to the youth and lay audiences of the country, would scarcely be expected to pose the same aesthetic problems (or situation) to the composer writing a work for the first clarinetist of one of our major symphony orchestras. On the basis of the composer's having accomplished what he set out to do, the Clarinet Concerto is a completely successful work.

The Heiress

During November and December 1948 Copland was in Hollywood, composing the score for the Paramount Pictures production of *The Heiress*. Based on the Henry James novel

[4] *op. cit.*, p. 252.

Washington Square, the film was directed by William Wyler and starred Olivia de Havilland. As a reflection of the 1850s, the setting of the story, Copland incorporated a number of popular examples of salon music of that era into his score. In addition he provided his own pastiche pieces appropriate for the period. Each of the leading characters was given a musical motif which undergoes transformation as the personalities develop during the story. This factor and the fragmentary nature of the film score make the music unsuitable for a concert suite so that it remains unpublished. In spite of a disagreement with the producers who replaced Copland's original title music with an orchestral arrangement of a French song that appears later in the film, the score received the Hollywood Academy Award for the best scoring of a dramatic or comedy production of 1949.

Preamble for a Solemn Occasion

Commissioned in 1949 by the National Broadcasting Company to commemorate the adoption by the United Nations of the Declaration of Human Rights, *Preamble for a Solemn Occasion*, originally entitled *Hymn*, sets the opening text of the United Nations' Charter for narrator and orchestra. (An alternative version omits the narration.)

The *Preamble* opens with a powerful unison theme on trumpets and trombones, characterised by wide melodic leaps (Ex. 97). This is taken up by the strings and woodwind

Ex. 97

and developed on full orchestra. The central section is a contrasting chorale on the upper wind, which prepares for the entry of the speaker. The text is treated in a similar manner to *Lincoln Portrait* with the phrases allocated to individual bars for free declamation against sustained chords on the strings and wisps of melody on solo woodwind and muted brass. The coda following the speaker's final words is an integration of the opening theme and the chorale in weighty chords. Although the work lasts only six minutes, the conclusion is as powerful as those of at least two major works, *Symphonic Ode* and the Third Symphony. It breaks no new ground but is an appropriate public utterance 'for a solemn occasion' and reveals Copland's ability to provide the right music for the right situation with no loss of integrity or craftsmanship. The orchestral score includes an alternative version of five bars if the speaker's part is omitted. The organ transcription dating from 1953 omits two bars before adopting the alternative version.

VIII. Vocal Music

(1949–1952)

After completing the *Preamble*, Copland turned from orchestral music to concentrate upon setting words. Of his next seven projects, only the Piano Quartet does not involve the voice.

Twelve Poems of Emily Dickinson

Copland composed solo songs at various times during his career, but not until 1950 did he complete a major vocal work. *Twelve Poems of Emily Dickinson*, written between March 1949 and March 1950, is not only his most important set of songs, but one of the most significant song-cycles of any composer of this century. He parallels the compactness of the poems with an economy of musical resources both in the directness of the vocal line and the relative simplicity of the piano part.

Emily Dickinson (1830–1886) was born in Amherst, Massachusetts and, except for a brief period away at school, spent the whole of her life in that town. After what seems a normal upbringing for the time, in her early twenties she experienced a severe (unrevealed) emotional crisis. As a result she retired to the seclusion of her home, and remained a recluse until her death at the age of 55. Only a handful of her 1,775 poems were published during her lifetime, and not until 1951 was a complete edition made available.[1] Since then, they have exerted a profound influence upon American composers as their direct expression and brevity make them eminently suitable for musical setting. Dickinson's writings were in essence a record of her thoughts on various subjects: life and death, love and nature. The strange personality of this remarkable woman

[1] *Complete Poems of Emily Dickinson*; ed. Thomas H. Johnson, Belknap Press of Harvard University, Massachusetts/Faber, London, 1951.

has given rise to extensive scholarly investigation of both her life and work.[2]

Copland wrote of his *Twelve Poems of Emily Dickinson* in a programme note:

> The poems centre about no single theme, but they treat of subject matter particularly close to Miss Dickinson: nature, death, life, eternity. Only two of the songs are related thematically, the seventh and twelfth. Nevertheless, the composer hopes that, in seeking a musical counterpoint for the unique personality of the poet, he has given the songs, taken together, the aspect of a song cycle. The twelve songs are dedicated to twelve composer friends.

In addition to the melodic relationship of two songs mentioned by the composer, the cycle possesses a unity

Ex. 98

beyond the common authorship of the poems. The interval of a third, so much a feature of Copland's melodic invention, especially in vocal lines (in, for example, *The Second Hurricane*), recurs throughout the work. A falling sequence of fourths, a further hallmark of the composer, and leaps of sevenths and ninths for the singer also provide an aural link between the separate songs. The piano writing is predominantly lean and linear, much of the time confined to single notes in each hand, with a customary economy of material.

Dickinson provided no titles for her poems, and so it has become customary to take the opening line as the title, a practice adopted by Copland, except for the last song

---

[2] To those wishing to learn more on the subject I recommend the exhaustive two-volume biography by Richard B. Sewall, *The Life of Emily Dickinson*, Belknap Press of Harvard University, Massachusetts, 1974/Faber, London, 1976.

('Because I would not stop for Death') which is called 'The Chariot'.

I. 'Nature, the gentlest mother'.
For this nature poem, Copland uses brief decorative figures on the piano to suggest bird-song. The vocal line is permeated with the interval of a third in a gentle pastoral mood (Ex. 99).

Ex. 99

II. 'There came a wind like a bugle'.
The violence of the poem is prepared by the piano scales in ninths and a bugle-call which is echoed in the opening vocal line (Ex. 100). The turbulence of a storm in the real world is

Ex. 100

the outward manifestation of a disturbance in the poet's mind. The piano depicts the quivering grass in rapidly alternating right-hand semi-quavers, and the booming bell in the church steeple with accented notes in the left hand. Intervals of seconds and ninths emphasise the violent agitation of the words.

III. 'Why do they shut me out of Heaven?'.
Copland sets this child-like, whimsical poem with an opening and closing declamation surrounding a more lyrical central section (Ex. 101). Thirds and falling fourths are much in evidence throughout this setting.

Ex. 101

IV. 'The world feels dusty'.

The two-note rocking figure in the accompaniment creates the feeling of a lullaby, a tranquil acceptance of death.

V. 'Heart, we will forget him'.

This sad poem of resignation is one of many that has led commentators to believe that the poet suffered from a tragic love-affair which left a permanent scar. The falling fourths (Ex. 102) emphasise the sense of loss.

Ex. 102

VI. 'Dear March, come in'.

In direct communion with elemental forces, the poet addresses the month of March, welcoming the return of spring. The exhuberant piano in $^6_8$ representing the activity of the season contrasts with the $^2_4$ rhythm of the voice in a breathless dialogue (Ex. 103).

Ex. 103

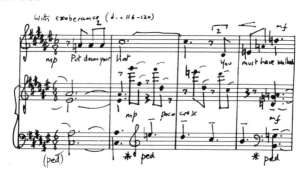

VII. 'Sleep is supposed to be'.
The emotional heart of the cycle, this song marks the end of
the first part; the composer asks for a long pause before the
following song. The austerity of the music underlines the
strange remote quality of the poem. The phrases of both the
vocal and piano parts are created from arpeggios.

At the climax, Copland marks both voice and piano *fff*
(Ex. 104).

Ex. 104

VIII. 'When they come back'.
A second spring-song in the form of an uncomplicated
diatonic vocal line against a continuous counter-melody on
the piano. The repetition of the opening phrase for each
verse hints at a strophic setting, but there is no exact repeat
of other figures.

IX. 'I felt a funeral in my brain'.
Marked 'heavy, with foreboding', this the darkest of the
poems reveals Emily Dickinson in a mood of depression. In
the piano part are heard the funeral tread, the beating of a
drum, and the doom-laden tolling of a bell. The unease of
the poet is underlined in the way that the tonality of the
vocal line is at odds with the chords on the piano (Ex. 105).
Here again are the falling fourths that Copland reserves for
moments of despair. And the tonal ambiguity of the final
bars suitably expresses the void depicted in the closing lines
of the poem, 'And I, and Silence, some strange Race
wrecked, solitary, here . . .'. (Copland omitted the final
stanza of the original poem.)

Ex. 105

X. 'I've heard an organ talk sometimes'.

In contrast to the unease of the previous song, the piano chords, in imitation of an organ, restore an air of calm. The contrary motion of the harmony in bars 3 and 4 (Ex. 106) has a modal flavour to conjure up the archaic association of a cathedral. And the arch-like shape of the vocal phrases evokes the architecture of a church.

Ex. 106

XI. 'Going to Heaven'.

The poem is a re-interpretation of 'Swing Low, Sweet Chariot', transformed by Emily Dickinson into a personal expression of her fundamental religious doubt. The naive confidence of the first line, given a rising melodic phrase, is balanced by the falling figure of mistrust (Ex. 107). As the assurance of salvation evaporates, the music becomes fragmentary and the upward melodic motive of the opening has become a mere echo in the closing bars.

Ex. 107

XII. 'The Chariot' ('Because I would not stop for Death').
At the outset, Copland recalls the opening bars of the
seventh song which contemplates sleep. In this poem the
writer seems to be in a dream, travelling with Death across
the countryside, past a school, cornfields and a homestead.
The dotted rhythm here suggests the carriage of Death
which 'We slowly drove – He knew no haste'. The quiet
calm of the music (Ex. 108) sustains the visionary
atmosphere of the poem; fear of death has been assuaged by
the hope of eternity.

Ex. 108

At several points in the song cycle, Copland requires the
third or middle sustaining pedal of a Steinway grand piano.
The effect allows certain notes to sound on after being
depressed, while subsequent notes played are not
sustained. In Ex. 109, taken from the last song, only the
semibreve notes in the first bar remain undampened.

Ex. 109

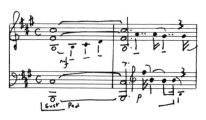

Between 1958 and 1970 Copland orchestrated eight of the
songs under the title *Eight Poems of Emily Dickinson*, which
were presented at the Juilliard School on the composer's
seventieth birthday. He omitted III, VIII, IX and X and
arranged the accompaniment for chamber orchestra of

single woodwind and brass, harp and strings, with the addition of an E flat clarinet.

Old American Songs

The two sets of *Old American Songs* (1950 and 1952) for voice and piano mark a return to a more popular style. The original tunes came from several sources, principally the Harris Collection of American Poetry and Plays at Brown University, Providence, Rhode Island.

First Set

I. 'The Boatmen's Dance'. This banjo melody by Dan D. Emmett, the composer of 'Dixie', was published in Boston in 1843.

II. 'The Dodger'. This satirical campaign song dates from the 1880s during the Cleveland-Blaine presidential campaign. It was sung by Mrs Emma Dusenberry of Mena, Arkansas, to John A. and Alan Lomax who included it in

Copland as Visiting Lecturer in Irving Fine's composition class at Brandeis University, Massachusetts, in the Spring of 1961; Fine is on Copland's left (photo courtesy of Verna Fine).

their collection *Our Singing Country*. The accompaniment imitates a banjo.

III. 'Long Time Ago'. Published in 1837 this sentimental ballad, probably of English origin, was arranged by Charles Edward Horn, the composer of 'Cherry Ripe', and George Pope Morris.

IV. 'Simple Gifts'. This famous song of the Shaker Sect, "'Tis the Gift to be Simple', dates from 1837. Copland had already used the melody for a sequence of variations in *Appalachian Spring*.

V. 'I Bought me a Cat'. Copland first heard this children's song from the playwright Lynn Riggs, who remembered it from his childhood in Oklahoma.

Second Set

I. 'The Little Horses'. This children's lullaby was published in the Lomax collection, *Folk Song USA*.

II. 'Zion's Walls'. The words and music of this revivalist song were composed by John G. McCurry, compiler of *The Social Harp*. Copland used the melody in his opera *The Tender Land* on which he was working at the time. There it forms the basis for the ensemble 'The Promise of Living'.

III. 'The Golden Willow Tree'. Also known as 'The Golden Vanity', this Anglo-American ballad is based on a recording made by Justus Begley in 1937 for Alan and Elizabeth Lomax.

IV. 'At the River'. Dating from 1865, this hymn-tune was composed by the Rev. Robert Lowry.

V. 'Ching-a-ring Chaw'. This minstrel song comes from the Harris Collection.

These arrangements preserve the melodies in their original forms with attractive accompaniments. Copland's expertise is seen in each of them with his customary economy of means. Both sets were subsequently arranged by the composer for medium voice and small orchestra.

IX. The Piano Quartet and 'The Tender Land'
(1950–1955)

Concert audiences were by this time more experienced and more receptive to modern music than had been the case twenty years before. In a sense they had caught up with the language Copland had abandoned after *Statements* in 1935 in favour of works using folk-song as basic material. The presence of Schoenberg, who had been teaching in California since 1934, had established the twelve-note technique among American composers. It was natural that at some time Copland should return to this most abstract of methods.

Piano Quartet
The Quartet for Piano and Strings (1950), commissioned by The Elizabeth Sprague Coolidge Foundation, marks the beginning of this return. It is based on an eleven-note serial row and is harmonically most closely related to the *Piano Variations*. The structure of the row with descending and ascending whole-tone phrases (Ex. 110) avoids the usual

Ex. 110

chromatic element of atonal music. The first movement, *Adagio serio*, opens with the tone-row presented fugally: violin, viola, cello, with the piano offering it both in inversion and a bar later in the left hand in its original form. A brief *stretto* on all instruments leads to the second subject on cello (Ex. 111), a retrograde version of the row, also shadowed canonically a bar later on the piano. The entire movement is based on the row; the descending and ascending whole-tone lines make the row easily recog-

Ex. 111

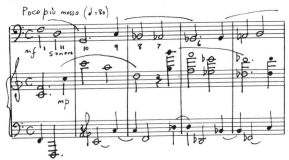

nisable by ear, even in elaborate transformation. But the canonical treatment of the theme and the clear implication of tonal centres distances the music from the Second Viennese School. Instead the first movement is closer to Bartók than to any serial composer, and the closing bars, with a return to a simple statement of the original theme, recall Bartók's 'arch' form. (Curiously, Copland's customary octave transposition of notes of a theme, an integral part of the atonalist's vocabulary, makes no appearance in the first movement.)

The second movement, *Allegro giusto*, is a scherzo in modified sonata-rondo form. Four rising tones appear in the first bar, balanced by five descending tones, the last two transposed up an octave (Ex. 112). These two phrases

Ex. 112

provide most of the material for the movement. Much of the piano writing for the first 50 bars is in octaves. The instrument is treated on a par with the strings; seldom is its weight used to counter-balance the other three players. Chords are rare, so that the contrapuntal writing creates a five-part texture. The first episode, introducing chattering quavers on the violin and piano, returns later with an accompaniment that suggests a dance tune, in the context surprisingly similar to a hoe-down (Ex. 113). The tone-row

Ex. 113

there also reappears as a reminder of the origin of the melodic invention. A passage of 24 bars in which the piano maintains a rhythmic ostinato accompanying the strings also recalls Bartók, especially where the violin and viola are required to pluck notes so that the string snaps onto the finger board. After a powerful chordal passage involving all four instruments, the coda by contrast is hushed, with fragments of the thematic material tossed from one instrument to another (*con sordino*) as the movement fades away to silence.

The finale is predominantly slow with several changes of tempo. The first section is for the strings without the piano (Ex. 114). The piano enters with repeated three-note phrases taken from the first notes of the row (resembling 'Three

Ex. 114

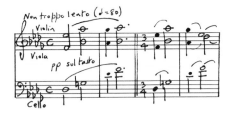

Blind Mice') against which the strings continue sustained melodic lines derive from the second bar of the movement. After a transformed version on the piano of the first subject of the movement, the strings introduce a chorale-like tune the opening outline of which resembles the first bar of the slow movement. Against this chorale, the piano maintains bell-like descending phrases. The relationship of the chorale to the original tone-row becomes evident when Copland combines the two (Ex. 115), with the piano re-introducing the opening theme of the movement. In the

closing bars over a pedal-point in the left hand of the piano,
Copland reiterates the three descending tones on the viola,
cello and piano, while the violin plays the sustained theme
from earlier in the movement.

Ex. 115

In the Piano Quartet, Copland's economical use of basic
material is seen at its most acute. The melodic ideas of all
three movements stem from the initial note-row theme,
especially the four descending tones of the first phrase. Of
this adoption of a form of serialism, Copland explained:[1]

> The attraction of the method for me was that I began to
> hear chords that I wouldn't have heard otherwise.
> Heretofore I had been thinking tonally, but this was a new
> way of moving tones about. It freshened up one's technique
> and one's approach. To this very day that remains its main
> attraction for me.

In spite of the serial nature of the theme, there is little in
common with the usual practices of atonal composition,
since a strong tonal sense is inherent in the note-row and its
subsequent treatment. It is among the most accessible of

[1] *Perspectives on American Composers*, ed. Benjamin Borentz and Edward T. Cone,
W.W. Norton, New York and Princeton University, 1971, p. 141.

the composer's absolute works and deserves a much wider recognition than it has currently received.

The Tender Land

To celebrate the 30th anniversary of the League of Composers in 1953, Richard Rodgers and Oscar Hammerstein II commissioned from Copland an opera, *The Tender Land*, to a libretto by Horace Everett, the pseudonym of a professional painter whose identity is still unrevealed. After the premiere in April 1954, when it was badly received, Copland and Everett made revisions to improve the dramatic elements of the plot and provide increased opportunity for development of the principal characters. With a revised first act, it was presented at Tanglewood on 2 and 3 August of the same year. Copland again withdrew the score to produce the final extended version in three acts instead of the original two; in this form it was staged in May 1955.

For the first performance, Copland provided this synopsis:

> The opera takes place in the Thirties, spring harvest time. It's about a farm family – a mother (Ma Moss), a daughter (Laurie) about to graduate from High School, her sister of ten (Beth), and a grandfather (Grandpa Moss). Two drifters (Martin and Top) come along asking for odd jobs. The grandfather is reluctant to give them any, and the mother is alarmed because she's heard reports of two men molesting young girls of the neighbourhoood. Nevertheless, they sleep in the shed for the night. The graduation party begins the second act. The heroine has naturally fallen in love with one of the drifters. And they prove it by singing a twelve-minute love duet. But there is something of a complication. You see, she associates him with freedom, and he associates her with settling down. Martin asks Laurie to run away with him, but in the middle of the night he decides that this kind of roving life is not for Laurie, so he silently steals off. When Laurie discovers she's been jilted, she decides to leave home anyway, and at the conclusion the mother sings a song of acceptance that is the key to the opera. In it she looks to her younger daughter as the continuation of the family cycle that is the whole reason for their existence.

The musical language belongs to that of the three popular ballets and the scores for *Our Town* and *The Red Pony*. The simple melodic fragment of the opening bars (Ex. 116)

Ex. 116

recurs as a motto evoking a pastoral scene of tranquillity on the Mid-West farm. Ma Moss, seated on a rocking chair in the porch and sewing, sings what could be a folk-song (Ex. 117). The three verses reveal the hardship of her life-work,

Ex. 117

the cold of winter and worries over her children. She is making a dress for Laurie's graduation the next day. Preparations for the party that evening reveal the pride that the family feels for the occasion. Laurie's song (Ex. 118)

Ex. 118

introduces the first hint of conflict. She sees beyond the graduation ceremony, dreaming of the future and the lure of life beyond the farm.

But little by little it came to be
That line between the earth and sky
Came beckoning to me.

What makes me think I'd like to try
To go down all those roads beyond
That live above the earth and 'neath the sky.

The scene between Laurie and her mother, inserted into the
final version, establishes the girl's resentment of her grandfather's over-protective authority. The itinerant farm-
workers, Top and Martin, resemble George and Lennie in
Steinbeck's *Of Mice and Men*; and Copland's score for the
film, dating from 1939, captures an atmosphere similar to
The Tender Land.

The music for the two drifters has a harder edge,
delineating the roughness of their characters. Their
conversation is delivered in a free and natural style in a
mixture of recitative, sometimes spoken, and brief lyrical
phrases. Their duet, 'We've been north, we've been south',
is suitably aggressive and masculine, accompanied
forcefully by the brass of the orchestra. Open fifths, fourths
and seconds emphasise their rough nature.

The alternation of recitative and lyrical melody is
achieved with a transition that preserves the realism of the
drama. The through-composed technique gives rise to brief
passages of quasi-folk-song which is the natural expression
of the characters.

The finale to the First Act, 'The Promise of Living', is
based on the revivalist song, 'Zion's Walls', that Copland
had incorporated into the second set of *Old American Songs*.
Like the quartet from Beethoven's *Fidelio*, the solo voices
enter one by one to build up a powerful ensemble of the five
principal figures in the opera (Ex. 119). The two distinct

Ex. 119

(a)

melodies are presented separately at first, and later combined. It is the most sustained and uplifting moment in the work and in the words of Julia Smith is 'the finest concerted piece of the entire opera'.[2]

Act II is set later in the evening of the same day. The graduation-eve party is well under way as the company finishes dinner. Laurie replies shyly to the toast in her honour with a touching aria that again expresses her dream of what is to happen in the future:

> This whole year it seemed
> The end point of my life was graduation.
> That was what my Ma and Grandpa had dreamed of,
> What I had dreamed of.
> What comes after? None could tell me;
> No one knew for sure.

To avoid a discussion of the vexed question of her daughter's future, Ma Moss invites the guests to dance. While the room is prepared, Top sets out to distract the grandfather so that Martin can court Laurie. Everyone except Top and Grandpa joins in the square dance, 'Stomp your foot upon the ground' (Ex. 120). Copland is here at his rhythmically most invigorating, a choral and orchestral counterpart to the 'Hoe-down' in *Rodeo*. A show-stopper of

Ex. 120

[2] *op. cit.*, p. 218.

exhausting vitality, it galvanises those on stage into frantic
activity which must set the audience tapping their feet. The
mood changes abruptly to a slow waltz as Ma Moss begins
to suspect the two drifters. She sends one of the guests to
fetch the Sheriff. Top, quite unsuspecting of the danger,
sings the folk-song 'Oh, I was a-courtin' and I knew just
where to go', the melody and words adapted from Cecil
Sharp's *English Folk Songs of the Southern Appalachians*,
published in 1917. Top does not realise the irony of the
words, 'In comes the old man with a double-barrelled
gun. . .'. Laurie and Martin detach themselves from the
dancing and go onto the porch. Their duet expresses quiet
tenderness in expansive slow lyrical melody (Ex. 121).

Ex. 121

At the point when everything seems idyllic, the lovers are
interrupted when Grandpa and Ma Moss burst in to accuse
Martin and Top of being the two men reported to have
molested innocent girls in the locality. Only the
intervention of the Sheriff explaining that the culprits have
been arrested earlier in the day prevents violence, but the
joy of the graduation party has been shattered. Grandpa
orders the two drifters to depart at daybreak and the guests
retire, leaving Ma Moss in despair alone on the stage.

Act III reveals Martin later that night in an agitated state,
outside the shed. Laurie also unable to sleep, comes out of
the house and pleads with Martin to be able to leave with
him in the morning. Their duet begins *sotto voce* but builds
up to a climax that ought to wake the entire household.
Martin is full of doubts but is eventually persuaded to take
Laurie with him. (This scene was added in the revision,
providing a more convincing explanation for Laurie's final

determination to leave her home.) When Top hears of this, he explains the stupidity of such a plan:

> That's crazy.
> Hoppin' the freight,
> After it's late,
> Sleepin' in a railroad crate.
> Is that how you see Laurie?

He understands Martin's deep feelings, showing sympathy in his persuasive appeal to make him change his mind. This is Top's finest moment, combining a strength of character with warmth of friendship for his companion. As daylight comes, Top and Martin creep off unheroically, shortly before Laurie excitedly emerges from the house, full of naive, girlish expectation.

> The sun is coming up,
> As though I'd never seen it before,
> The day is bright and clear.
> The door I've just come through
> Has opened on a new earth,
> A new land.

Her horrified discovery of Martin's departure provides Copland with his final dramatic outburst; dissonant chords on the full orchestra emphasise her despair in a style familiar in Hollywood film music (Ex. 122). Laurie recovers

Ex. 122

from the shock with remarkable self-possession, resolving to leave home for some unknown destination. This is the crux

Working with Leonard Bernstein in January 1964 in New York (photo courtesy of CBS Records).

of the story; she has graduated not only from school, but from childhood. She ignores the entreaties of her mother, who realises that she can no longer hold Laurie at home. Ma Moss accepts that her daughter must discover the world for herself. The opening music of the opera returns in the closing pages as Ma Moss turns to Beth as her hope for the future.

In *The Tender Land* Copland succeeds in creating believable personalities with genuine human feelings. He avoids the stylisation of grand opera and the artificiality of the musical, an achievement accorded to few composers of this century. Julia Smith summed up its qualities thus: '*The Tender Land* is sincere, indigenous, gay, lusty, at times powerfully beautiful, poignantly nostalgic and emotionally moving'.[3] And Andrew Porter has commented: '*The Tender Land* is a Midwestern idyll – not a realistic drama but a romantic, pastoral folk tale'.[4]

In 1957 the composer arranged a concert suite from *The Tender Land*, first performed in April of the following year. The suite begins with music from the Introduction to Act III, leading to the love duet, virtually complete. The dance music of Act II provides the lively central section, and 'The Promise of Living' quintet concludes the excerpts.

[3] *op. cit.*, pp. 220–221.
[4] *Music of Three Seasons*, Farrar, Straus and Giroux, New York/Chatto and Windus, London, 1979, p. 288.

Dirge in Woods

Copland's most recent song for voice and piano, *Dirge in Woods*, to words by George Meredith, was composed in honour of the fiftieth anniversary of Nadia Boulanger's teaching career. In spirit it is closest to the Emily Dickinson Songs, with tonal ambiguities throughout, in spite of a key signature implying E flat major. Appropriately, the first performance was given at the Fontainebleau School in the Summer of 1954, with the New York premiere taking place in Spring 1955.

Canticle of Freedom

Canticle of Freedom for chorus and orchestra was commissioned by the Massachusetts Institute of Technology for the dedication of the Kresge Auditorium in Cambridge, Massachusetts, and was performed at the dedication ceremonies in May 1955. The text is taken from the poem *Bruce*, written about 1375 by the Scottish poet John Barbour (1316–1395). Copland set a short excerpt extolling the idea of freedom. The words of the original are in Middle Scots but the composer used a modern equivalent. *Canticle of Freedom* is not a choral work in the customary form, since the choir does not enter until more than half-way through. In the revised version, published in 1967, Copland shortened the orchestral introduction but the proportions still suggest an orchestral piece with a choral ending.

The opening line of the chorus (Ex. 123) provides the

Ex. 123

thematic germ of most of the melodic invention of the orchestral introduction. After the powerful opening bars, on brass, wind and percussion, the figure in Ex. 124 is heard on

Ex. 124

flutes. There is a progressive increase in tempo with each
new section. A counter theme on brass (Ex. 125a) is related
to a phrase (Ex. 125b) heard later in the chorus. A further

Ex. 125

statement of the motto theme on woodwind and trumpet
leads in a central development section which prepares for
the entry of the choir. A three-note rising figure (Ex. 126a),
also on woodwind, has its counterpart later in the chorus
(Ex. 126b). Each new phrase for the chorus is presented in

Ex. 126

unison before treatment in four-part harmony. The
concluding bars for the full forces are in Copland's characteristic ceremonial vein. *Preamble for a Solemn Occasion* is its
closest companion, but this work is on a larger scale, lasting
approximately thirteen minutes.

X. Instrumental Music and 'Dance Panels'
(1955–1962)

In 1955 a commission jointly from the Boston Symphony Orchestra, to celebrate their 75th anniversary, and the Koussevitzky Music Foundation offered the composer the opportunity to revise the *Symphonic Ode* of 1929. This is discussed above (pp. 47–53) along with the original version.

Piano Fantasy
Copland's third major keyboard work, the *Piano Fantasy*, was begun in 1955 and completed in 1957. It was commissioned by the Juilliard School for its 50th anniversary and dedicated to the memory of William Kapell. It is cast in a single movement of large proportions, lasting half-an-hour, and makes use of serial techniques. Copland wrote:[1]

> A long and continuous one-movement form has always seemed to me one of the most taxing assignments a composer can undertake. The largest problem is to give free rein to the imagination without loss of coherence – to be 'fantastic' without losing one's bearings. My idea was to attempt a composition that would suggest the quality of fantasy, that is a spontaneous and unpremeditated sequence of 'events' that would carry the listener irresistibly (if possible) from first note to last, while at the same time exemplifying clear, if somewhat unconventional, structural principles.

Although the initial basis of the *Piano Fantasy* is serial, tonal orientation pervades the music. The 'row' comprises four descending and six ascending notes widely spaced, the first four repeated (Ex. 127). The forceful declamatory opening is balanced by a slow *cantabile* melody in the right hand

[1] On the sleeve note to the Unicorn recording, RHS 323.

Ex. 127

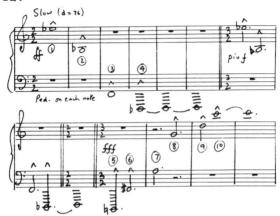

against a quiet sustained chord in the left hand (Ex. 128). A three-note figure dominates almost every bar of the third

Ex. 128

section, marked 'Rubato, restless, hesitant', which becomes progressively more agitated. This, too, is balanced by a more tranquil passage of a quieter, pastoral nature, mostly in four-part chords (Ex. 129). At its simplest it is reduced to

Ex. 129

two-part bitonality with a three-chord figure in the left hand, resembling classical horn-writing of fifths, sixths and thirds, which recurs at several points in the work.

The central section of the *Fantasy* is an extensive virtuosic scherzo mostly in two-part dialogue or unison between the two hands. The additive rhythmic patterns create frequent changes of time signature, with notes flying past like lightning. The headlong rush of music recalls two works of the 1930s, the *Piano Variations* and *Short Symphony*. The 'trio' of this scherzo, marked 'twice as slow, with humor', is in playful mood, fragmented into short phrases in the right hand against sustained or single notes in the bass. The return of the scherzo is no mere repetition, but a continued development of the original material. It is briefly interrupted with a return to the pastoral music earlier in the work. The scherzo closes with wild scales and *glissandi* in the right hand against the widely spaced note-row in the left hand.

The final section is based on the opening pages, no literal recapitulation but with sufficient close reference for the ear to note a sense of return. The intricate part-writing is notated on three staves to delineate the separate lines to be clearly articulated. The music of the coda is a slow, quiet unwinding of the intensity that has marked many of the earlier episodes. The second subject re-appears almost unaltered to herald the marked simplicity of the close in contrast to the complexities of the central scherzo. The final bars (Ex. 130) present a form of the note-row in contrary motion, ending on a characteristic Copland chord in the depths of the piano keyboard.

Copland's piano-writing exploits the extreme ends of the piano. At one point near the beginning, four staves are employed in order to simplify the reading of widely spaced part-writing. Throughout there is a sense of spontaneity within a carefully structured form. More than in any of his other works the composer inserts frequent instructions to the performer, sometimes indicating fluctuations in both tempo and mood – 'hurried and tense', 'soft and clear', 'delicate, uncertain', 'gradual return to poetic, drifting', 'r.h. freely accompanying (not too precise), l.h. controls tempo with exactitude', 'sotto voce, muttering', 'with mounting excitement', 'no tone whatsoever'. All these reveal Copland's desire for accuracy of expression.[2]

By any standards, the *Piano Fantasy* is a major keyboard work of this century, offering a rewarding challenge for a pianist with sufficient technical resources and musical insight.

Ex. 130

In 1956 Copland took on a new and increasingly important career as a conductor, not only of his own works but also of those of other Americans. In this role, for over twenty years, he paid frequent visits to Europe, Japan, Australia, Israel and Russia, in addition to extensive tours of the United States. He had made his debut as a conductor with the Orquesta Sinfónica de México in 1947, performing the Third Symphony. In his autobiographical sketch[3] he reported:

> An elderly and wise woman once gave me some excellent advice, 'Aaron,' she said, 'it is very important, as you get older, to engage in an activity that you didn't engage in when you were young, so that you are not continually in

---

[2] The discussion between Aaron Copland and Leo Smit on the piano music printed in Appendix I (pp. 197–212) examines these instructions further.

[3] *The New Music 1900–1960*, p. 165.

With Walter Piston at Dartmouth College, Hanover, New Hampshire, in August 1967.

competition with yourself as a young man.' The conductor's baton was my answer to that problem.

He has continued this activity, even conducting at concerts for his eightieth birthday in the United States and London. A valuable legacy of recordings of his music under his direction has been created, mostly for CBS, with almost every orchestral item and several of the chamber works included in the series. Exceptions to date are the early *Cortège macabre*, Symphony No. 1, *Prairie Journal* and *Canticle of Freedom*. Orchestral players speak highly of his powers of communication both in words and with the baton. Rehearsals are relaxed but business-like; the London Symphony Orchestra in particular built up a special relationship with him which has led to highly successful concerts and recordings.

Orchestral Variations

In 1957, to a commission from the Louisville Orchestra, Copland orchestrated the *Piano Variations*. The composition of the *Piano Fantasy* no doubt renewed his interest in the *Variations*, to which it is closely related. The revision of the *Symphonic Ode* also drew him back to earlier music, and the potential of the *Variations* as an orchestral work led him to look at it in a different light.

The *Orchestral Variations* is a remarkably successful composition in its own right, offering new opportunities to explore orchestral sonorities with powerful results. Copland uses the standard full orchestra of double-woodwind with some doubling (two piccolos, for example), four horns, two trumpets, three trombones, tuba, timpani, harp and strings. The only 'extravagance' is in the percussion section, where two players cover thirteen instruments.

A comparison of the orchestral score with the original piano version reveals little additional material, except when a few imitative voices were inserted where the texture might have been too thin. It is interesting to note features of scoring that resemble passages from early orchestral works. For example, in the final variation an ostinato figure is repeated in semiquavers on cellos and quavers on double-basses which do not coincide; in the finale of the First Symphony a similar feature appears between timpani and double basses. And although the closing bars resemble the final passage of the First Symphony, they also anticipate the grinding dissonances of *Connotations*, a work composed thirty-one years after the *Piano Variations* but only four after the *Orchestral Variations*.

The World of Nick Adams
Also in 1957, Copland provided incidental music for Columbia Television to accompany a production of Ernest Hemingway's story *The World of Nick Adams*.

Nonet
Copland's Nonet for Strings (1960) was commissioned by the Dumbarton Oaks Research Library, Washington, D.C., in honour of the 50th wedding anniversary of Mr and Mrs Robert Woods Bliss, and is dedicated to Nadia Boulanger 'after forty years of friendship'. Although composed for three violins, three violas and three cellos, it can be played by proportionally larger forces, but not by the normal string orchestra. The scoring is the same as for Bach's Third *Brandenburg* Concerto but with no double-bass.

In the Nonet Copland returns to diatonicism although retaining the use of certain serial methods. The work is in a

basic A–B–A form, and in the slow-fast-slow plan resembles
the *Piano Fantasy* in structure. The opening three chords
(Ex. 131) provide the basic material for the first part. The

Ex. 131

entry of two violas in canon a few bars later bring to mind
Bartók's method of building up a slow but intense accumu-
lation of contrapuntal parts with a gradual crescendo. An
expressive tension arises from the heavy scoring with
individual lines emerging through the texture. After the
climax the opening chords return quietly on the full
ensemble. In the bridge passage which leads to the central
scherzo, the first violin interpolates a new melodic figure
(Ex. 132), the modality of which suggests plainsong
intonation. The scherzo is built on typical fragments

Ex. 132

exchanged between the instruments in ever-changing rhythmic patterns and time-signatures. The melodic outlines are
related to the 'plainsong' theme heard earlier. This theme
also emerges on the violas and cellos as a counter-subject to
the scherzo figures, at times in augmentation. The instruments are treated principally as nine separate soloists but at
certain points Copland groups them, like Bach in the
opening movement of the *Brandenburg* Concerto No. 3, in
answering phrases (Ex. 133). It is at this point that another
work associated with Dumbarton Oaks comes to mind. The
slotting of two bars of $\frac{7}{16}$ into the otherwise regular crotchet
pulse may be a conscious reference to Stravinsky's Concerto
in E flat for Chamber Orchestra, *Dumbarton Oaks*: it had been
Mr and Mrs Bliss who had commissioned *Dumbarton Oaks*,

and Nadia Boulanger who, in Stravinsky's absence through illness, had conducted its premiere.

Ex. 133

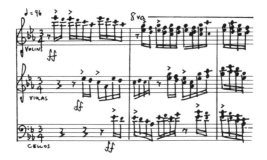

A rhythmical figure is developed towards the end of the scherzo which allows the momentum to slacken through a transition to the slow tempo of the opening. The cyclic nature of the work is evident when the musical ideas of the opening section return in reverse order. After a passage of chords played *tremolando sul ponticello*, the 'plainsong' theme re-appears, again on violins. The coda recalls two of Copland's earlier compositions for strings, the *Two Pieces* for string quartet of the 1920s and the third of the *Statements*. The two-chord figures at the end of the latter are particularly close in character to a similar passage in the Nonet. And Copland ends the Nonet in customary style, with the opening three-chord phrase now extended by a very slow tempo (Ex. 134).

Ex. 134

With Samuel Barber in Barber's studio in his house 'Capricorn', Mount Kisco, New York, on 3 March 1968 (photo by Phillip Ramey).

The composer has commented:[4]

> The medium itself (three violins, three violas, three cellos) is rather severe, and also, one might say, bottom heavy, because the violas and cellos tend to overweigh the lighter quality of the violins. This makes for a somewhat solemn sound, grim at the beginning and athletic in the middle.

The opening and close are elegiac in mood, but by no means gloomy. The interplay of rhythmical and contrapuntal ideas in the central section provides an extreme contrast with lively exchanges between the instruments.

The infrequency of performances of the Nonet arises from the technical problems presented to the players and the unusual choice of ensemble, more difficult to assemble than the two string quartets required for Mendelssohn's Octet or the six players for the two Sextets, Opp. 18 and 36, of Brahms. For the listener it is an approachable work, clear in form and exciting in execution.

[4] Sleeve note to the CBS recording M32737 (not issued in the UK).

Down a Country Lane

In response to a *Life Magazine* commission in 1962 Copland composed *Down a Country Lane* for piano. In 1965 he scored it for performance by school orchestras. This brief pastorale resembles the simplicity of *Our Town*.

Dance Panels

In 1963, on a commission from Jerome Robbins, Copland completed his latest ballet, *Dance Panels*, begun as early as 1959 and revised in 1962. Cast in seven sections, it has no specific scenario, and the composer has allowed choreographers to interpret it in abstract terms or with a story. It is scored for medium-size orchestra, with only one each of oboe, bassoon and trombone. Copland provided the following commentary:

> *Dance Panels* was conceived as a ballet without a story. The published score is not a suite from the ballet but the entire music. Stylistically *Dance Panels* is direct and comparatively simple – some parts are very diatonic, 'white-notey', one might say. The lyrical music is certainly plain, without complexities of texture. Portions of the score are quite lively and bouncy. The Introduction, with long, sustained notes, is in slow waltz tempo. The second section continues the waltz rhythm and is followed by the third, a light transparent scherzando. The fourth part is a melancholy and nostalgic pas de trois, while the fifth is characterised by brisk rhythms and jazzy drum patterns. The sixth section is a lyrical episode and, after a finale in jagged, irregular rhythms, the work ends as quietly as it began.[5]

Most of the opening section consists of long sustained notes, except for a brief trumpet call (Ex. 135). The second

Ex. 135

---

[5] Sleeve note to the CBS recording M33269 (73451 in the UK).

*Listening to a playback at the CBS studios in London, around 1970
(photograph by Julian Hann, courtesy of CBS Records).*

'Musingly': Copland photographed in 1970 by Viktor Kraft.

section is a slow lyrical waltz, with frequent pauses (Ex. 136). It is one of the few passages similar to the pastoral moments in the three 'cowboy' ballets. But neither the melodic nor rhythmic ideas elsewhere in *Dance Panels*

Ex. 136

suggests a Western setting; there are no quasi-folk-songs or country dances. The scherzando which follows without a break is derived thematically from a widely spaced figure heard on flutes, in the previous section. The similarity here is not with a ballet, but with the fifth movement, 'Jingo', of *Statements*. The transition based on the trumpet call leads to Section IV, *Pas de Trois, lento,* ('somewhat hesitant, melancholy and naive') which is dominated by a sad melody on an alto flute (Ex. 137). The lively fifth section highlights

Ex. 137

the percussion (side-drum, suspended cymbal played with a brush, wooden block, temple blocks). Melodic figures are fragmentary and nervous in character (Ex. 138). In the sixth

Ex. 138

section an expressive melody on woodwind and strings is accompanied by rapid repeated four-note phrases derived from the previous movement. The violent ending prepares for the final section, *molto ritmico*, whose principal material is based on upward scales, often harmonised in seconds. The coda is based on the trumpet fanfare and sustained notes of the introduction, ending on an isolated clarinet.

XI. Serialism

(1962–1968)

Although Copland had grown up musically aware of the innovations of Schoenberg, Berg and Webern, experiencing their works first-hand through the ISCM Festivals in the 1920s, their atonality had virtually no impact upon his own method of composing.

> I was interested and fascinated by them. I did not go along with the expressive character of their music. It still sounded very 19th century and highly romantic. That was just the thing we were trying to get away from.[1]

Until the 1960s, *Poet's Song* of 1927 and the Piano Quartet of 1950 are the only pieces that show any extensive influence of the twelve-note system. It was therefore received with some surprise that, like Stravinsky in his seventies, Copland in his early sixties should turn to serialism in the next two orchestral works.

Connotations

To celebrate the opening of the Philharmonic Hall (now Avery Fisher Hall) in the Lincoln Center in 1962, the New York Philharmonic Orchestra commissioned *Connotations*. The *Concise Oxford Dictionary* defines 'connote' as to 'imply in addition to the primary meaning'. In Copland's work the note-row is the primary meaning, and the subsequent treatment of it explores the implications which lie within it.

Connotations is an essay in contrasts which do not destroy the inherent unity: the chordal writing gives way to outbursts of complex counterpoint, and the melodic lines with wide leaps and arpeggios, often incorporating ninths, resemble similar figuration in the *Short Symphony*, completed some thirty years earlier. Nor is it surprising that Copland should imitate the rhythmic patterns of the

---

[1] 80th-birthday interview with Alan Blyth, BBC Radio 3, 14 November 1980.

Symphonic Ode since he revised that work in 1955. In programme notes for the first performance, the composer explained his intention behind the music.

> I decided to compose a work that would bring to the opening exercises a contemporary note, expressing something of the tensions, aspirations and drama inherent in the world today. In *Connotations* the row is first heard vertically in terms of three four-voiced chords with, needless to add, no common tones. When spelled out horizontally, these chords supply me with various versions of a more lyrical discourse.
>
> Structurally the composition comes closest to a free treatment of the baroque form of the Chaconne. A succession of variations, based on the opening chords and their implied melodic intervals, supplies the basic framework.

Copland employs a large orchestra: three flutes, piccolo, two oboes, cor anglais, four clarinets (including E flat and bass clarinet), two bassoons, double-bassoon, six horns, four trumpets, four trombones, tuba, timpani, piano, celesta, a large percussion section and strings. For the first time in a Copland score, all transposing instruments are written in C,

Sir Michael Tippett, Phillip Ramey and Copland at Tippett's home in Corsham, Wiltshire, in September 1967.

with the usual octave transposition for piccolo, glocken-spiel, double-bassoon and double-basses. This facilitates the tracing of the note-rows and their transpositions.

Like the *Symphonic Ode*, also a single-movement work, *Connotations* is structurally in the form of an arch in five sections. The first section has a chordal opening, and is predominantly slow; section two is a scherzo; section three emerges from the scherzo and is in a slower tempo; section four is a return of the scherzo; and section five balances the opening with certain passages taken from the first part.

As stated above, the note-row is heard first in three four-part chords on two trumpets and two trombones. These are separated by repetitions of the chords on the remaining trumpets and trombones introducing simultaneously a significant rhythmical element (Ex. 139). The third chord is

Ex. 139

the same as the second, but transposed up a tone. The row is presented twice, the second time transposed up an augmented fourth with a different distribution of notes within each chord. By presenting the 'row' in this way, the sequence of the note-order is ambiguous, since within each chord the notes can be numbered from the top or from the bottom. In a characteristic way, Copland punctuates the end of this statement with two emphatic chords, repeated after a silent bar, one long, one short, of extreme dissonance and unusual spacing (Ex. 140). To establish the chords firmly, as much for the listener as for the music itself, they are repeated several times in various transpositions. The first episode retains chordal features in a less rigid chorale-like manner.

As in the *Orchestral Variations*, Copland is obsessed with the interval of a minor ninth, which originates from the second and third chords of the work. In a later passage for

Ex. 140

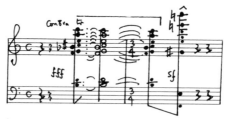

woodwind (Ex. 141), closely related to the chorale, these
ninths appear in almost every chord.

Ex. 141

An eloquent melody which follows at bar 36 (Ex. 142) on
oboe, cor anglais, trumpet and violins embraces all the
twelve semitones except one (A natural). In this respect the

Ex. 142

melodic development is close in character to Schoenberg in
his Violin Concerto. In a way seen in the *Symphonic Ode*,
Third Symphony, and *Orchestral Variations*, Copland
introduces short semiquaver fragments on the woodwind
against the passacaglia-like music of the strings, until the
orchestration is reduced to these figures alone in a playful
decoration above the simple cello line (Ex. 143).

Ex. 143

The three note-row chords recur in various forms throughout the work. Each newly created melodic line is derived from the notes of the chord in correct order (Ex. 144).

Ex. 144

That Copland should imitate the rhythmic patterns of the *Symphonic Ode* is not surprising, since he revised the work in 1955, but it is noteworthy that some melodic and rhythmic development closely resembles passages in the first movement of the *Short Symphony* completed some thirty years earlier.

The scherzo is interrupted by another Schoenberg-like melody in which the note-row is again strictly observed. But even in this atonal work, rhythmic and melodic traits of Copland's diatonic music recur. The oboe figure in Ex. 145,

Ex. 145

(a) Connotations

(b) Third Symphony

with short balanced phrases, recalls the middle section of the second movement of the Third Symphony. And a strong theme in double counterpoint (Ex. 146), again traceable to the notes of the row, indicates the enormous range of musical ideas which can emanate from so simple a source.

Ex. 146

The coda brings back music heard earlier as a summary of
the principal ideas of the work. *Connotations* closes with a
now familiar gargantuan climax of sheer weight and noise,
noted before in other works – especially in the First
Symphony, Piano Concerto, *Symphonic Ode*, the Third
Symphony and the *Orchestral Variations*. In this instance
Connotations transcends all these for violence and
dissonance, created not only by the harmony, in which all
twelve semitones are sounded simultaneously, but by
flutter-tonguing flutes, trumpets and horns, reinforced by a
formidable barrage of percussion that includes a metal plate
and tam-tam played *fff*. This is the loudest orchestral noise I
have ever encountered in the concert hall.

Music for a Great City

In 1961 Copland composed the score for the film *Something
Wild* based on Alex Karmel's novel *Mary-Ann*, starring
Carroll Baker and produced by Jack Garfine. The music
provides an aural portrait of New York City, the setting of
the film. When the London Symphony Orchestra requested
a work from Copland in the following year for their 60th
anniversary season, he drew on the film score for the
commission. *Music for a Great City* was begun in 1963 and
completed in April 1964. The composer explained in a
programme note for the premiere in London:

> The nature of the music in the film seemed to me to justify
> extended concert treatment. No attempt has been made in
> 'Music for a Great City' to follow the cinematic action of
> 'Something Wild'. The four movements of the work alternate
> between evocations of big city life, with its external stimuli,
> and the more personal reactions of any sensitive nature in
> the varied experiences associated with urban living. 'Music

In Venice in October 1967, with the Rialto Bridge behind him (photo by Phillip Ramey).

for a Great City' reflects both of these aspects of the contemporary scene.

It is scored for the standard large orchestra, with Copland's customary large percussion section employing seven players for nineteen different instruments. The four movements have the titles 'Skyline', 'Night Thoughts', 'Subway Jam' and 'Toward the Bridge'.

'Skyline': the powerful dissonant opening chords in full orchestra portray the towering buildings of New York. The percussive nature of the subsequent music suggests the noise of traffic and the incipient violence of the city. Jazzy ostinati emphasised by an imposing array of percussion (snare drum, tenor drum, conga drum, wood-block, cowbell, sandpaper, xylophone, vibraphone, glockenspiel and piano) make it clear that we are in America. A central passage of contrasting lyricism briefly arrests the aggressive onslaught. Snatches of pastoral melody on woodwind and strings suggest the peaceful oasis of Central Park amidst the busy streets (Ex. 147). The respite is brief before a return of the forceful opening music which seeks to overwhelm us. After the final chord of this movement with flutter-tonguing brass, the second movement is a welcome relief.

Ex. 147

'Night Thoughts': a melancholy theme repeated several times (Ex. 148) establishes a sombre atmosphere, although

Ex. 148

even here the mood becomes restless with a sudden cry of pain (Ex. 149). The tone of the also flute reinforces a pervading sadness.

Ex. 149

'Subway Jam': scored for wind, brass and percussion, this movement is explicit in its depiction of traffic. Trombones conduct an extended dialogue with five percussionists. Shades of Bartók's *Miraculous Mandarin* are close at hand, with uncompromising dissonance. The entry of the woodwind brings a temporary lessening of tension, but the full brass take the movement to a battering climax.

'Toward the Bridge': much of the material resembles the first movement. In a work short on melody, a theme on the bassoon near the beginning (Ex. 150) stands out as an expression of humanity in a hostile world. Then the bustle of the city returns with a characteristic coda for full orchestra marked *ff*, based on the opening bars of the work.

Ex. 150

Emblems

In May 1963, Keith Wilson, President of the College Band Directors' National Association asked Copland to compose a work for concert band. He wrote: 'The purpose of this commission is to enrich the band repertory with music that is representative of the composer's best work, and not one written with all sorts of technical or practical limitations'.

Copland began work on *Emblems* in the summer of 1964 and completed it in the following November. It is scored for the full forces of the American band, including E flat, alto and contra-bass clarinet, separate cornets and trumpets, piano, and an array of percussion distributed among four players. Copland adopts his familiar tripartite form: slow–fast–slow, with a varied return to the music of the opening. Throughout, his stylistic finger-prints appear: the opening bars, in characteristic monumental vein, juxtapose fanfare-like figures between brass and woodwind. This powerful introduction recalls the *Symphonic Ode* and *Preamble*, with a balance between unison and harmonised phrases. Exchanges of four-note motifs on varied instrumental groups lead to an extended melody on a solo oboe (Ex. 151). And in places the introduction quotes the hymn tune 'Amazing Grace'.

Ex. 151

The central *allegro* is built on spiky fragments, lightly scored in a rapidly changing kaleidoscope of instrumental colour. And the modified return of the opening slow music, using the full forces builds up to a typical Copland blazing finish. In a foreword to the score, the composer explains:

An emblem stands for something – it is a symbol. I called the work EMBLEMS because it seemed to me to suggest musical states of being: noble or aspirational feelings, playful or spirited feelings. The exact nature of these emblematic sounds must be determined for himself by each listener.

In the summer of 1965 Copland was the narrator in a memorable performance of *The Soldier's Tale* at a Stravinsky Festival at Philharmonic Hall, New York, with John Cage as the Devil and Elliott Carter as the Soldier; and in 1966, in response to a commission from CBS, Copland composed the theme music for CBS *Television Playhouse*, to be used as an introduction to each drama production.

Inscape
The 125th anniversary of the New York Philharmonic Orchestra in 1967 gave rise to commissions for eighteen composers, both American and European. Among those invited were Richard Rodney Bennett (Symphony No. 2), Elliott Carter (Concerto for Orchestra), Howard Hanson (Symphony No. 6), Roy Harris (Symphony No. 11), Gunther

Outside the Teatro Comunale in Bologna, where Copland conducted a concert of Busoni (who spent two unhappy years as director of the Accademia Filarmonica there), Schubert, Copland and Ives, in October 1967 (photo by Phillip Ramey).

Schuller (*Triplum*) and Roger Sessions (Symphony No. 8). Copland's contribution, *Inscape*, was first performed in September. The title is taken from the English poet Gerard Manley Hopkins (1844–1889), for whom the word 'inscape' suggested 'a quasi-mystical illumination, a sudden perception of that deeper pattern, order and unity which gives meaning to external forms'.[2] Copland has stated[3] that *Inscape* is more relaxed than *Connotations*:

> With *Inscape*, I allowed myself more tonal implications within the twelve-tone procedure. There is quite a lot of two-voice writing that suggests tonalities; I felt that two voices would tend to imply chords where more might suggest tone-clusters. Two different series of twelve-tones provide the materials from which it derives a major proportion of the entire composition. One of these dodecaphonic tone rows, heard as a 12-tone chord, opens and closes the piece. Ultimately *Inscape* like *Connotations* reflects, to some degree, the tenseness of the times in which we live.

In his study of 20th-century musical trends[1] Arnold Whittall explains the desired effect of Copland's use of serialism:

> For Copland himself, as his comments on *Inscape* show, the ultimate hope may be for tonality to survive revitalized 'by a fusion' with twelve-note technique: for tonal implications and directions to emerge from twelve-note writing.

The forces required are less than those for *Connotations* – standard full orchestra of triple woodwind, four horns, three trumpets, three trombones, tuba, harp, piano, celesta, timpani, percussion (four players) and strings.

The first tone-row is heard as a single chord: the notes read from bottom to top provide the sequence in Ex. 152;

Ex. 152

[2] W.H. Gardner, *The Poems of Gerard Manley Hopkins*. Penguin Books, Harmondsworth, 1953, p. xxi.

[3] In a sleeve note for the CBS recording (73198).

[1] *Music since the First World War*, J.M. Dent, London, 1977, p. 92.

the final C sharp is omitted initially. In contrast the second
row is presented as lyrical two-part dialogue on the
woodwind (Ex. 153).

Ex. 153

The melodic aspect provides a stronger tonal direction in
Inscape than in *Connotations*. Except for brief phrases of
two-part writing, there is virtually no contrapuntal development, with a notable conformity of crotchet movement in
the melodic lines. Only in the central section is there a
rhythmical development of quavers with one episode of
irregular time-signatures. Octave or unison doubling of
two-part writing helps to reinforce the tonal implications of
melodic lines and intervals.

Inscape is a reflective, gentler counterpart to the more
extrovert and aggressive *Connotations*. Demands on both
players and listeners are fewer, making it a useful
introduction to its longer, more complex companion.

XII. Late Works
(1969–   )

Following the completion of *Inscape*, Copland experienced increasing difficulty in writing music. With the exception of the Duo for flute and piano, all the works from this time are short in duration and in many cases reworkings of unpublished pieces initially written several years earlier.

Happy Anniversary
For Eugene Ormandy's 70th birthday in 1969, Copland wrote *Happy Anniversary*, like Stravinsky's *Greetings Prelude* a brief orchestral tribute based on 'Happy Birthday to You'.

Ceremonial Fanfare & Inaugural Fanfare
Also dating from 1969 are two fanfares: a *Ceremonial Fanfare* for full orchestral brass was commissioned by the New York Metropolitan Museum in celebration of its Centennial Year; and the *Inaugural Fanfare* for concert band was commissioned by the City of Grand Rapids, Michigan, for its new City-County Plaza in Vandenberg Center, and the unveiling of Alexander Calder's stabile 'La Grande Vitesse'. The score of the latter was revised in 1975.

Duo
The Duo for flute and piano was composed on commission from a number of pupils and friends of William Kincaid (1895–1967), for many years principal flute in the Philadelphia Orchestra. In the Duo Copland returned to the 'simple' tonal, harmonic, and melodic language of the Violin Sonata. In a conversation with Phillip Ramey, the American composer and writer, he provided the following description:

> It is a lyrical piece in a somewhat pastoral style. Almost by definition, it would have to be a lyrical piece, for what can you do with a flute in an extended form that wouldn't emphasize its songful nature? Of course you could write

fancy effects for a while, but, to my mind, lyricism seems built into the flute. If one decides to write a work for flute, I think that that, in itself, is a kind of limitation and should be taken into account.

The first movement opens with a solo passage for flute. Before long, the music picks up momentum and, after what might be termed a development of the fast section, returns in reverse order to the music of the opening pages. The middle movement is the least complex, both formally (a three-part structure) and from the standpoint of melodic construction. I think it came off well because it has a certain mood that I connect with myself – a rather sad and wistful mood, I suppose. The last movement, in free form, is in strong contrast, because it is lively, bright and snappy.[1]

All three movements have a basic A–B–A form. The first is in Copland's customary arch structure; it begins on the unaccompanied flute with fragments of modal melody in short phrases often of three notes, in the form of a rise and fall (Ex. 154). When the piano appears, it accompanies the

With Roy Harris in San Francisco in June 1969, after a rehearsal of Harris' Third Symphony with the San Francisco Symphony Orchestra under Copland (photo by Phillip Ramey).

[1] In the sleeve note to the CBS recording (M32737).

Ex. 154

soloist in a melody (Ex. 155) that could have come from *Appalachian Spring.* As the tempo quickens, the opening short phrases become extended into flowing melodies

Ex. 155

interchanged between the two instruments. The subsequent running semiquaver scales in the flute recall similar music on flute and piccolo in the third movement of the Third Symphony. A new dotted rhythm (Ex. 156) is introduced,

Ex. 156

suggestive of dance music. As the tempo slackens, the material of the opening returns in a varied form. The slow movement, marked 'Poetic, somewhat mournful', is characterised by an almost constant pedal point in the left hand of the piano, which emphasises a funereal tolling of a bell.

Against this, the flute unfolds a free melody which is independent of the piano, both in tonality and rhythm; its plainsong-like modality seems to imply word-setting.

The central section is the emotional heart of the work, with an intensity of expression on the flute in its high register; as in the previous movement, it closes with an adapted return of the opening bars. The finale, which follows without a break, changes the solemn mood to one of vitality. It is a modified rondo in the style of a lively dance. This also has its roots in the popular ballets (Ex. 157).

Ex. 157

Threnody I in memoriam Igor Stravinsky
Following the Duo, there was a gap of more than two years before Copland completed his next work, *Threnody I in memoriam Igor Stravinsky* for flute and string trio. Dated 19 September 1971, it appeared first in the Boosey and Hawkes periodical *Tempo* as one of several musical tributes from a number of composers. Subsequently the composer made a slight revision of the music providing an additional seven bars introduction before the entry of the flute. This miniature, lasting only two minutes, is cast in the form of a canonical passacaglia on the strings, while the flute laments in a free flow of melody. No doubt Stravinsky would have admired the economy embodied in this simple exercise of counterpoint (Ex. 158).

Ex. 158

Threnody II in memoriam Beatrice Cunningham

Threnody II in memoriam Beatrice Cunningham, dated 1973 and composed to commemorate the death of a personal friend, is a more extended and intricate work. Scored for alto flute

Ex. 159

and string trio, it is based on a tone-row (Ex. 159), first heard after the introduction on an unaccompanied viola. This is balanced by the retrograde version on unaccompanied also flute. The central section builds up an emotional tension using melodic lines derived from the tone-row. As often with Copland, the coda is an adapted repetition of the opening bars.

Three Latin-American Sketches

In 1959 the Festival of Two Worlds in Spoleto, Italy, asked Copland for a short orchestral work. Although the *Two Mexican Pieces* were completed in time, only the second of them, 'Danza de Jalisco', was performed at the Festival in July of that year. Both pieces, the first, entitled 'Paisaje Mexicano' ('Mexican Landscape'), were heard at a concert of the Pan-American Union in Washington in April 1965, conducted by the composer. Still not satisfied with them, in 1971 Copland added a further piece, 'Estribillo', based on a popular song from Venezuela, making some revisions in 'Danza de Jalisco' for the two-piano version. The three pieces were re-issued in 1975 under the title *Three Latin-American Sketches*. In an introductory comment on the record sleeve[2] the composer said:

> I would describe the character of the *Three Latin-American Sketches* as being just what the title says. The tunes, the rhythms and the temperament of the pieces are folksy, while the orchestration is bright and snappy and the music sizzles along – or at least it seems to me that it does. Nevertheless, the *Sketches* are not so light as to be pop-concert material, although certainly they would be a light number in a regular concert, much in the same way as *El Salón México*.

[2] CBS M 33269 (73451 in the United Kingdom).

Conducting the Radio TV Orchestra in Bucharest on 20 November 1969.

They are scored for a small orchestra, one each of the woodwind, a trumpet, two pianos (the second optional), one percussion player and strings. The first movement, 'Estribillo', most closely resembles *El Salón México* with its vigorous cross-rhythms in the two principal themes (Ex. 160). The colourful percussion, including claves, wood block, conga drum and ratchet, serve to underline the Mexican flavour. 'Paisaje Mexicano', the slow movement, is based on a song-like theme (Ex. 161) played in turn on each of the wind and the upper strings. The spirited finale, 'Danza de Jalisco', alternates bars of $\frac{6}{8}$ and $\frac{3}{4}$ (Ex. 162).

Ex. 160

Ex. 161

Ex. 162

Although a slight work in comparison with other orchestral pieces, the *Three Latin-American Sketches* reveal Copland's skill in using simple melodic material to maximum effect.

Night Thoughts

For the Van Cliburn International Quadrennial Competition held in Fort Worth, Texas, in September 1973, Copland was commissioned to provide a test piece for the candidates. After its completion, he gave *Night Thoughts* the subtitle *Homage to Ives* because the subtle use of piano sonorities by careful pedalling effects and the powerful, often dissonant writing is a reminder of the older composer. (There is no relationship with Copland's earlier 'Night Thoughts', the slow movement of *Music for a Great City*: this

Outside the Atheneul Roman, Bucharest's principal concert hall (photo by Phillip Ramey).

Visiting a Rumanian village on the arm of a government guide; the photographer Victor Kraft is on the left (photo by Phillip Ramey).

piano piece is 'mood music', while the orchestral 'Night Music' is a peaceful nocturne of quite different character.)

Cast in a single movement, the work is a study in textures: basically slow throughout, there are no sudden changes of tempo or character, each episode arising naturally from the previous one with slight fluctuations of speed. In the opening bars two of Copland's intervallic fingerprints appear: the melodic third and the harmonic ninth. These recur throughout. The first three notes provide a unifying motto figure (Ex. 163), at times harmonised

Ex. 163

bitonally between the two hands. As in other works, phrase lengths are short, usually of one bar. Only one more extended melody emerges (Ex. 164), and even this contains balanced repetition. Copland is meticulous in marking the

Ex. 164

pedalling; in the first seven bars, the performer is instructed to depress the pedal *after* striking each note. In the closing bars, the *sostenuto* pedal is required to maintain one chord through several changes of harmony. At times the music is written on three and four staves to accommodate the wide range of the keyboard used and to determine clearly the duration of sustained chords against overlapping melodic phrases.

In Evening Air & Midsummer Nocturne
Copland's last four published works are brief and wistful piano solos. *In Evening Air*, composed in 1966 and published in 1972, was commissioned by the Scribner Music Library.

In mood it looks back to the pastoral music of *Our Town*. The title is taken from lines by Theodore Roethke:

> I see, in evening air,
> How slowly dark comes down on what we do.

Midsummer Nocturne was composed in 1947 as part of an unfinished suite of simple piano pieces for children. It is dedicated to Phillip Ramey who discovered the manuscript in 1977 among the composer's personal documents.

Midday Thoughts & Proclamation

In 1982 he completed two short piano solos for Bennett Lerner who had played the Piano Sonata several years earlier. *Midday Thoughts* is based on sketches of a slow movement for piano and orchestra dating from 1944. *Proclamation* was begun in 1973. Both pieces were first performed by Bennett Lerner in Carnegie Recital Hall, New York on 28 February 1983.

At Peekskill in 1983, correcting the proofs of Midday Thoughts *with Bennett Lerner for whom it, like* Proclamation, *was composed (photo by Phillip Ramey).*

Proclamation for Orchestra

In late 1984 Copland, who was ill at the time, asked Phillip Ramey to orchestrate the piano piece *Proclamation*. Ramey did this early in 1985, for performance by Zubin Mehta and the New York Philharmonic in New York on 14 November 1985, at an all-Copland concert to celebrate the composer's 85th birthday (with Bennett Lerner, for whom the original version of *Proclamation* had been written, as soloist in the Piano Concerto), and, a few hours later, by Erich Leinsdorf and the Los Angeles Philharmonic in California.

XIII. Postscript:
Style and Language

The most consistent stylistic feature of Copland's music is the economy of thematic material. In a wide range of pieces, from the Piano Trio *Vitebsk* and the *Piano Variations* to *The Red Pony* Suite, the Clarinet Concerto, *Piano Fantasy* and the late Duo for flute and piano, three-note figures are sufficient for extensive development. Elsewhere, balancing phrases of four and five notes predominate in his compositions; the themes of all four movements of the Third Symphony, for example, have these characteristics.

The melodic interval of a third, major and minor, is a fingerprint that recurs regularly, appearing frequently in the *Dance Symphony*, Organ Symphony and the Piano Concerto, *Vitebsk*, *Appalachian Spring*, the Violin Sonata, Third Symphony, the Emily Dickinson Songs, *Dance Panels* and *Night Thoughts*. With hardly an exception, the tunes in his school opera *The Second Hurricane* are constructed on the repeated interval of a third. Themes built on arpeggios (which inevitably include thirds) are also a significant feature of pieces from all periods including the *Dance Symphony*, the Emily Dickinson Songs, *Piano Fantasy* and the serial *Connotations*. Continuous thematic development confined solely to crotchets and minims also characterises the opening of several works: *Piano Variations*, the first *Statement* ('Militant'), *Symphonic Ode*, *Preamble* and *Emblems*. This is heard at its most extreme in *Inscape* where the first quavers do not appear until bar 50 and are not thereafter re-introduced until bar 70.

In spite of occasional bitonality in *Statements*, *Billy the Kid*, and *In The Beginning* and the use of serial techniques in the *Piano Variations*, Piano Quartet, *Piano Fantasy*, *Connotations* and *Inscape*, his harmonic language is basically diatonic. At times the melodies and their accompanying harmonies are modal in character.

In the absolute works he creates the formal structure

through the alteration of short melodic fragments by repetition and extension. The adjective 'spare' is often applied to the textures that result. As Joseph Machlis says:

> Like Stravinsky he uses as few notes as possible. The careful spacing of the chords is a delight to those who examine his scores. His spare instrumental writing emphasizes the high registers, particularly of the trumpets and violins. This helps him achieve the clean, transparent sound that is one of the hallmarks of his style.[1]

The deeply ingrained influence of hymn-tunes that has affected the more overtly nationalistic of American composers might be considered the original but indirect source for the hymn-like melodies of the cosmopolitan Copland. Although his music is undeniably American, the inclusion of folk-songs (apart from the *Old American Songs* which are deliberate arrangements) is confined to the three popular ballets, the *Lincoln Portrait* and, to a very limited extent, *The Tender Land*, where direct association with the setting and subject is established by quotation. In that opera and the Third Symphony, the melodies have a folk-song flavour but are nevertheless original. *El Salón México* and the *Three Latin-American Sketches* are isolated cases, since they are designed as a tribute to the music of another country. Arthur Berger says: 'It might even be said, with a certain irony, to be sure, that Copland has had more influences on American folk music than it has upon him'.[2]

Similarly, the influence of jazz in work of the 1920s has been absorbed into his own language and in no way represents pastiche or mere imitation. Its syncopated rhythm and irregular accents had a lasting effect throughout his composing career.

What, ultimately, is the essential quality of Copland's music which distinguishes it from that of other major figures of this century? Often the outsider is in the best position to assess clearly and objectively the true nature of a composer who epitomises what is American. Two English

---

[1] *Introduction to Contemporary Music*, 2nd edition, W.W. Norton, London & New York, 1979, p. 390.
[2] *op. cit.*, p. 93.

Copland with composer David Diamond at Copland's Peekskill home on 24 May 1985 (photo by Phillip Ramey).

writers have concisely summarised what Copland has achieved:

> There is no music which conveys the big-city experience more honestly than Copland's: which is more compassionately human in its acceptance of spiritual isolation: or which attains through it, through tension, a deeper calm.[3]

> There is an over-mastering sense of good humour and downright optimism; rare and welcome qualities today. The tone of voice is sometimes jaunty, sometimes tender, sometimes harsh, sometimes unashamedly rhetorical.[4]

And from the American standpoint, Harold Schonberg has written:

> Councelor and elder statesman, Aaron Copland is the urbane, respected symbol of half a century of American music.[5]

In *The New York Times* to mark Copland's 50th birthday, Olin Downes wrote:

> His music is the expression of an urban composer, grown up in the crowded city and in the period in which America has

[3] Wilfrid Mellers, *op. cit.*, p. 101.
[4] Desmond Shawe-Taylor, *The Sunday Times*, London, 15 November 1970.
[5] *The Lives of Great Composers*, Davis-Poynter, London /W.W. Norton, New York, 1970, p. 505.

changed from an agricultural to a predominantly industrial civilization. Copland's sense of style is that of the American who is of his country, his time, his environment, at the same time that he is spiritually a man of the world, in touch with all the currents of thought from overseas and the sophistication of the European Schools of composition.[6]

I leave the final tribute to his friend Virgil Thomson who, as early as 1948, described him in a *New York Herald-Tribune* article as 'a national glory'.[7]

[6] 29 October 1950.
[7] 'On Being American', 25 January 1948; reprinted in *A Virgil Thomson Reader*, p. 305.

XIV. Copland the Writer

As an author Copland brings to his writings the directness and lucidity found in his compositions. Behind the literary style is the same careful construction, the avoidance of superfluous expression and economy of means. The first of his four books, *What to Listen for in Music*, appeared, significantly, at a time shortly after he had written *El Salón México*, *Billy the Kid* and other works intended for a wider audience. At the outset, he explained his intention: 'To put down as clearly as possible the fundamentals of intelligent listening to music is the object of this book'. The popularity of radio and records was producing a rapidly increasing musical public which required guidance. In 1928 Walter Damrosch began his influential series of musical appreciation broadcasts for NBC radio, and Copland's own public lectures on modern music at the New School for Social Research in New York date from this time. Without condescending to the amateur, he sought in his book to present the composer's view, not merely of his own work, but of all music:

> The layman always finds it hard to realize how natural it is for the composer to compose. He forgets that composing to a composer is like fulfilling a natural function.[1]

He sets out to define the four elements of music, the composer's 'materials': rhythm, melody, harmony and tone-colour. On the subject of consonance and dissonance he states:

> Dissonance is only relative to you, your epoch and the place it holds in the piece as a whole. If all new music sounds continually and unrelievedly dissonant to you, then it is a safe guess that your listening experience is insufficient as regards music of your own time.[2]

[1] *What to Listen for in Music*, McGraw-Hill, New York, 1939, p. 19.
[2] *ibid.*, pp. 46–47.

Leonard Bernstein, Phillip Ramey, Copland and composer John Corigliano (far right) on the terrace of Ramey's New York apartment on 19 May 1982 (photo by Kenneth LaFave).

In subsequent chapters, Copland presents a succinct explanation of basic musical forms of the past, with a particular emphasis on understanding the question of musical style and interpretation. In the appendix he gives simple examples of variation formulas applied to the folk-song 'Ach, du lieber Augustin'. He traces the line of communication from the composer to the interpreter to the listener, with an acute insight into the personality of the composer and the influences upon him. There have been numerous books on musical appreciation, many of them effective and instructive, but Copland's is one of the first to explain the processes in music from the standpoint of the creator, although in a letter to Copland after the publication of *What to Listen for in Music*, Virgil Thomson expressed a sceptical view on the subject of the intelligent listener.

> Supposing that you do believe that analytic listening is advantageous for the musical layman, it is still quite possible and not at all rare to believe the contrary. It even remains to be proved that analytic listening is possible even. God knows, professional musicians find it difficult enough. I suspect that persons of weak auditive memory do just as well to let themselves follow the emotional line of a piece, which they can do easily, which they certainly can't do very well while trying to analyse a piece tonally. In any case, I find it a bit high-handed to assume the whole psychology.

Copland's second book, *Our New Music*, was first published in 1941 by McGraw-Hill in New York and re-issued in a revised and enlarged edition in 1968 by Norton in New York and Macdonald in London under the title *The New Music 1900–1960*. In this form it comprises a sequence of essays gathered into three categories:

I. Survey of Contemporary European Composers, 1900–60;

II. Composers in America;

III. The Present Day.

Many of these writings date originally from the 1930s, with additional observations in 1967 offering, in places, a change of attitude over the years. Often, however, he abides by the judgements made over thirty years earlier on contemporary figures. Some parts of the earlier book have been omitted where comments on radio, recordings and film were no longer relevant. Several essays are based on articles written for radio talks and lectures. The late-19th-century background and the exhaustion of post-Wagner German romanticism are presented as the reason for the need of a fresh start to the 20th century. Copland pays a special tribute to Mussorgsky as the most original of the Russian 'Five', and a prophet of the musical future. Schoenberg, Bartók and especially Stravinsky emerge as the primary composers in the first half of this century. Of Stravinsky he writes: 'He gave European Music what amounted to a rhythmic hypodermic. It has never been the same since'.[4]

From his own experience he describes the significance of the musical scene in Paris after the First World War. He is particularly revealing on the transitory influence of jazz upon serious composers. The dodecaphonic school of Schoenberg, Berg and Webern and late Stravinsky are seen from the situation in 1967 when their music had become more widely heard and accepted.

Of all writers on the subject, Copland is in the best position to describe the emergence of young composers in the United States. He explains the predicament of those who were attempting to discard the powerful influence of Europe:

[3] Paris, 20 March 1939; reprinted in (ed.) Gertrude Norman and Miriam Lubell Shrifte, *op. cit.*, p. 379.

[4] *The New Music*, p. 46.

Listening to a new piece by David Del Tredici (right) in Copland's home at Peekskill, New York; between them is the composer-pianist Robert Helps, in 1974 (photo by Phillip Ramey).

The simple truth is that no composer worthy of the name has ever written anything merely to be 'as great as' or 'better than' some other composer. He writes in order to say something of his own – to put down some expression of his own private personality.[5]

In a postscript of 1967 he expressed some misgivings over the increasing number of university campus composers who fail to make an impact on the wider musical public. A similar dilemma of communication had faced Copland in the 1930s, which led him to alter his approach to composition with a deliberate attempt to win audiences. Financially protected by a salary, the university composers are in danger of adopting an inward-looking approach that will lead to compositional sterility. In addition works written for particular performers involve such technical complexities and special treatment of instruments that musicians outside the specialist groups for which the pieces were written may be unwilling or unable to perform them. Such composers seldom touch what Copland calls 'the normal world of music makers and music listeners'.[6]

Hindsight allows the present-day reader of the essay on

[5] *ibid.*, p. 100.
[6] *ibid.*, p. 108.

Charles Ives, written in 1933, to be astonished at the insight into the music of a composer so little known and performed at that time: 'It seems safe to say that Ives was far more originally gifted than any other member of his generation'.[7] But even then Copland recognised the major weakness of Ives through his lack of self-criticism. His admiration for Roy Harris, Roger Sessions, Walter Piston, Virgil Thomson and Marc Blitzstein does not prevent his seeing their various shortcomings. The autobiographical sketch 'Composer from Brooklyn', written in 1939 for *The Magazine of Art*, remains the most vivid portrayal of his early years.

The final section, 'The Present Day', new in 1967, is a survey of the total serialism of Boulez and Stockhausen, the music of chance (John Cage) and the electronic media. Although showing a clear understanding and in part admiration for the *avant garde*, he is critical of certain aspects of their work:

> With reckless disregard for what players like to play, and for practicalities of the instruments, composers have been providing music that is, at times, playable by only a handful of specialists in contemporary music.[8]

With *musique concrète* and electronic music there is the danger that the engineer will take over from the composer:

> The basic sine tones produced by the generator have little tonal variety; consequently much tape music has a depressing sameness of sound.[9]

In conversation with Alan Blyth, Copland light-heartedly gave his reasons for avoiding *avant garde* media:

> I couldn't manage to write electronic music even if I wanted to because I've no mechanical talent. I feel thankful I am able to turn on an electric light switch. As for aleatoric techniques, I've spent my life trying to put the right notes in

[7] *ibid.*, p. 109.
[8] *ibid.*, pp. 180–1.
[9] *ibid.*, p. 186.

the right places so that I would find it too much of a violent
change to let things go their own way.[10]

In 1951 Copland was invited to deliver the Charles Eliot
Norton lectures at Harvard University. In the following year
the six lectures, entitled *Music and Imagination*, were
published in America by the Harvard University and in
Britain by the Oxford University Press. They are dedicated
to the memory of his brother Ralph (1888–1952). In the
Preface, Copland explains the structure of these lectures:

> The first half of the book treats of the musical mind at work
> in its different capacities as listener, interpreter, and creator.
> The second half discusses more specifically recent mani-
> festations of the imaginative mind in the music of Europe
> and the Americas.[11]

In the first lecture, 'The Gifted Listener', Copland extends
his exploration of the listening process, first introduced in
What to Listen for in Music. Again he emphasises the
importance of the art of listening:

> Listening is a talent, and like any other talent or gift, we
> possess it in varying degrees. I have found among music
> lovers a marked tendency to underestimate and mistrust this
> talent, rather than to overestimate it.[12]

Of his own reaction to music, he admits to a certain
detachment.

> Not infrequently I have been moved to tears in the theater;
> never at music. Why never at music? Because there is
> something about music that keeps its distance even at the
> moment that it engulfs us.[13]

In this respect Copland seems to agree with Stravinsky that
music is not a language of emotions but one which can be
understood only in musical terms:

[10] *The Times*, London, 14 November 1970.
[11] *Music and Imagination*, p. vii.
[12] *ibid.*, pp. 7–8.
[13] *ibid.*, p. 10.

No true music-lover is troubled by the symbolic character of musical speech; on the contrary, it is this very imprecision that intrigues and activates the imagination.[11]

He complains of the preponderance of old music in concert programmes, of a misguided reverence for the classics. Concert halls throughout the world have become 'musical museums'.

In the second lecture, 'The Sonorous Image', Copland explores the importance of sound. His own aural memory is strong enough for him to recall the exact sound of pieces of music heard many years ago, a phenomenon probably shared by both performing musicians and amateur listeners. The composer's concern for particular sounds is seen most acutely in orchestration. Copland has a high regard for Berlioz in his mixing of instrumental colours and for Ravel and Stravinsky as masters of the orchestra.

In the third lecture, 'The Creative Mind and the Interpretative Mind', he returns to his own attitude to composition.

Why is it so important to my psyche that I compose music? Why is the creative impulse never satisfied? I must create in order to know myself. Because of this each artist's work is supremely important – at least to himself.[15]

This is not a statement of self-justification from an egocentric artist but an honest attempt to explain to the layman the driving force behind the creative artist:

And just as the individual creator discovers himself through his creation, so the world at large knows itself through its artists, discovers the very nature of its being through the creations of its artists.[16]

In this way the composer is an interpreter of musical truths for the benefit of the listening public. He has an aesthetic obligation to communicate with others, not merely express

[11] *ibid.*, p. 13.
[15] *ibid.*, pp. 40–41.
[16] *ibid.*, p. 41.

Conducting in the 1960s (photos courtesy of CBS)

private, personal ideas with little or no meaning to anyone but himself.

The role of the performer beyond a technically accurate rendering of the composer's notes is of critical significance. His own personality will inevitably intrude so that his interpretation will necessarily differ from that of another fellow musician. This factor as such does not alarm Copland as a composer since different renderings of a piece can vary in character while remaining faithful to the composer's wishes. But he does lament once again the dilemma for the composer of today:

> For the most part, a regrettable gulf separates the inter-preter and composer in present day musical life.[17]

The fourth lecture, 'Tradition and Innovation and Recent European Music', outlines the conflicting trends in 20th-century music: neo-classicism which brought order to impressionism, the English tradition, the systems of Hindemith and especially the paradox of Schoenberg where a new discipline of the organisation of twelve tones has led to chaos and anarchy. Even more today than earlier in the century, it has to be asked 'for whom is the composer writing?', since new music now reaches a diminishing audience.

The fifth lecture, 'Musical Imagination in the Americas',

---

[17] *ibid.*, p. 57.

recounts the historical development of music in the New World, including Latin America, from its origin in 18th-century Europe, with Handel, Haydn and Mozart, to the present day. Copland is especially pre-occupied in tracing the use by American composers of small irregular units, so much a feature of his own work, to African and Spanish influences. The polyrhythmic setting of free rhythms against a steady pulse, the swing element of jazz comes from the same sources.

The final chapter, 'The Composer in Industrial America', examines the role of the American composer today, seen through Copland's own experience but enlarged to embrace a wide spectrum of others dating back to Paine, Horatio Parker, Foote and Chadwick. He expresses surprise that no-one has written a book on American serious composition which goes beyond biographical details. He reiterates the

Nearly 20 years later, Copland rehearses the London Symphony Orchestra on 1 December 1980 for his 80th birthday concert the following night (photographs by Malcolm Crowthers).

current dilemma facing the contemporary composer who must strive to appeal to an audience:

> The worst feature of the composer's life is the fact that he does not feel himself an integral part of the Musical Community.[18]

Copland on Music, his fourth book, published in 1961,[19] is a compilation of miscellaneous essays on music written over a span of thirty years. He provided pen-portraits of musicians associated with his career, including Nadia Boulanger and Koussevitzky, and American composers who were his contemporaries. In addition there are reprinted reviews of 20th-century music heard at European festivals. These collected writings conclude with an essay on the notation of rhythms, a problem Copland had encountered in his own compositions.

In the last quote above, Copland is speaking with regard to most living composers – but the verdict does not apply to himself today. His position in American musical life is stronger than that of any other composer at any time in the United States. Unlike many great artists, Copland has received well within his lifetime recognition for his contribution to music in America. Most of his works have been recorded under his direction, and throughout the world he is represented in concert programmes. His 80th birthday was celebrated with festivals in the United States and concerts and broadcasts in Europe and his 85th by an unprecedented, season-long retrospective of his music by the New York Philharmonic. The breadth of his musical language extends to the widest possible audience, from those who enjoy the simplicity of folk song to the sophisticated listener who prefers the absolute medium of serialism. Each will find in his music much to satisfy his taste.

---

[18] *ibid.*, p. 110.
[19] By Doubleday in New York and André Deutsch in London.

Appendix 1.
A conversation on the piano music

Aaron Copland and Leo Smit

Leo Smit and Aaron Copland were visiting artists at the 'Learning From Performers Program' at Harvard University on 1 November 1977. On the following evening Leo Smit gave the first public performance of the complete piano works that Aaron Copland composed from 1921 until then (*Midday Thoughts* and *Proclamation*, in their final forms, date from 1982).

Leo Smit (born in 1921) is a composer, teacher and pianist who has taught at the State University of New York, Buffalo, since 1962. Among his compositions are two symphonies and a piano concerto.

The following dialogue, which was printed on the sleeve of Leo Smit's two-disc recording of *The Complete Music for Solo Piano*,[1] is a slightly edited version of their conversation.

The sketches of Copland conducting which are interspersed throughout this Appendix by way of contrast with its subject-matter were made by Milein Cosman during rehearsals on the occasion of one of Copland's visits to London in the early 1970s.

AC: My first piano piece, *The Cat and the Mouse*, written in 1920, was composed in Brooklyn while I was still a student of Rubin Goldmark. I'm sorry to say Mr Goldmark has been rather forgotten as one of my teachers because of the glamor of the name of Nadia Boulanger, with whom I later studied in Paris for three years. But I worked with Rubin Goldmark for four years, and all that was the grueling part of compositional studies: basic harmony and counterpoint and lots of exercises – that sort of thing. It wasn't so much free composition. Mr Goldmark thought if you could write the first movement of a piano sonata, and do it well, that should be the apex of your ambition. I managed to do a whole

---

[1] CBS 79234. This album omits, at the request of the composer, *Sentimental Melody* (1926). Because this collection was released in 1979, it does not contain the two late works, *Midday Thoughts* and *Proclamation*; it also omits *Petit Portrait* (1921), published in 1981, and *Three Moods* (1920–21), published in 1982. All of these pieces, along with the unpublished *Sonnet II* (1919), have since been recorded by Bennett Lerner for Etcetera Records.

piano sonata which, today, I wouldn't show to anybody. But anyhow, *he* was pleased. And then I went on to other things.

I suppose you might want to know how a composer writes his music. And perhaps I should concentrate on the three largest piano works, namely, my Piano Sonata, my *Piano Variations* and my *Piano Fantasy*. All the other works are shorter, considerably shorter, and I don't think they pose any listening problems. And they range, of course, from *The Cat and the Mouse* to *Night Thoughts*, which was written in 1972. That's a span of more than fifty years. I don't know where all those fifty years went to. It doesn't seem to me as if it could possibly have been that long; but there it is, the dates on the pieces are definite proof. In between I wrote three works that I consider my main contribution to piano literature. First, the *Piano Variations* in 1930, then the Piano Sonata from 1939 to 1941, and then the *Piano Fantasy* in 1957. The *Fantasy* is by far the most ambitious of those three works. It lasts, I believe, a full half-hour without pause. It's a terrific trial for any pianist.

How you go about writing pieces like those three would be a legitimate question for anybody to ask. My answer is: you go about it by getting musical ideas that seem pregnant with possibilities for development. That's basically it. You might get a musical idea and think, oh, this is pretty – but what am I going to do with it? It doesn't seem to suggest any particular use. But an idea that seems to have within itself – for some reason or other, and there might be many different reasons – the possibility for development, for being combined with other ideas that seem nuggets of expressivity – those you hold on to for dear life. And, of course, you jot them down immediately so you won't forget them.

Now, I compose at the piano. I think that might be helpful when writing piano music. (It might be a hindrance if you don't know how to do it, and you try to write orchestral music at the piano.) It used to be thought rather shameful for a composer to admit that he used an instrument when he wrote his music. But one day Stravinsky said he *always* wrote at the piano, and then it became OK! But laymen are liable to be confused if you say you write at the piano. They visualize it this way: you go to the piano and by chance you put your hand down on a chord and think, oh, that's nice, I like that. And then, by chance, you happen on something else. But it doesn't quite work like that. It can't all be chance, can it? Something is guiding those ten fingers of yours. Because if it were just chance, you'd be chancy every day and you'd be likely to get nowhere. So there must be something that tells your ten fingers, or five or two or even one, if you are picking out a melody

that fascinates you – something in your brain is directing your fingers. After all, a musical idea is just a musical idea. If you're not a real composer with training to back you up, you won't know what to do with it. So that, even though you may use an instrument when you write, that doesn't solve the problem of how you put together a twenty-minute work, or a half-hour work like the *Piano Fantasy*, and that fact must be remembered.

But I suppose the foremost problem in the structure of a piece of absolute music that has no story content is truly one of the most challenging things the human mind can battle with. How the devil a piece that starts with a few notes here and, half an hour later, ends over there – how you put all those notes together so that they

seem to make a logical flow and seem to be concerned with a subject matter or a series of subject matters that appear to make sense together – that's very mysterious indeed, and the counter-point exercises you have and rhythmic studies, etc., will be a help, but they will not solve that final problem of putting a long and developed and seriously considered piece together from beginning to end, whether you write at the piano or at your desk or however you write it; the end result is always the result of a considerable amount of inspiration, calculation and knowledge – the things you were taught, the things you remember, the things you experience when you listened to music. An enormous amount of background is there for everything that you've created. Even a simple piece has to make sense. But the moment you start to get beyond the first two or three minutes of a piece of music you're creating, you face potential trouble. And if you're ambitious enough to write a work that lasts half an hour without pause, you're in very serious trouble, unless you can call upon a considerable amount of actual experience that you've had as a composer in writing works that you've heard in public performance. Because that's important, too: a piece that you play to yourself at home in your studio is one thing; but to sit and hear it with an audience is a different experience, and usually the piece doesn't sound quite the same as it does at home. It takes on a different sort of life. The long parts – the parts that you thought were perhaps too long – get their real test when they're played before an audience. Sometimes you think you did stretch it out a bit too much; sometimes you think it's too short. You get all sorts of reactions when you listen to your own music (I do, anyhow). And I think that would be characteristic of most composers, if they're able to free themselves sufficiently to think about their music as if somebody else had written it. That, too, is not easy to do. Many composers fall in love with their own works to such an extent that they lose all sense of critical objectivity. Composers vary greatly in their attitudes toward their own music.

At any rate, I've been trying to say that these three major pieces – all of my music for piano, in fact – were born at the piano. Sometimes they were asked for by a performer, sometimes not, but always they were based on pregnant material. Can we give an illustration of pregnant material?

LS: Beginning of the *Piano Variations*?

AC: How many variations are there? Have you ever counted them?

LS: Twenty, plus an extended coda.

AC: Well, you had twenty chances in other words to vary your theme. That's a lot of chances. And you can do quite a lot of different things with those few notes.

LS: I've always wanted to ask you but have been afraid to ask if, at the time of composing the *Variations*, you were in any way immersed in the music of Bach?

AC: No, I can't say I was.

LS: Because the notes with which you build the theme are exactly the same as those which Bach uses in his C sharp minor Fugue, *Well-Tempered Clavier*, Book I. A little out of order, but those are the notes. No connection?

AC: No. I had composers I was fond of. I have enormous admiration for Bach. But I never remember thinking: I am *now* being influenced by Bach.

The *Variations* somehow filled a special niche in my production. I think it was one of the first works where I felt that 'this is me' – that somebody else, taking the same theme, would have definitely written something different. That's only natural, but in my own mind, the piece had a certain 'rightness' about it. The *Variations* seemed to flow one after the other – varied, of course, each one different – but each one seemed to follow on the other. It took me about a year to write this ten-minute piece. It isn't that I worked on the *Variations* every day, of course. But it's very valuable to get away from what you are creating for a while, to forget about it, so that when you come back you can think about it freshly. That's extremely important because you tend to go stale – the mind starts bogging down if you stay with it continuously. I know there are certain composers who either have to compose their work all in one fell blow of inspiration or they can't do it at all. But I'm the other type who needs to get away for a while – because it always seems different when you come back and look at it again from a somewhat different point of view. You're in a different mood. You're either more critical or less critical, but it doesn't seem the same, and that's important because then you can go on and think about it in different ways. The *Variations* took a long time to write. I didn't write the variations consecutively. In other words, I got ideas for the variations and worked on them without having too clear a notion as to exactly where they were going to fit in the finished piece. And then on one fine day every variation seemed to run to its right place. That was, of course, a lovely day.

I think one of the satisfying aspects of the piece is that the *Variations*, in my own mind at any rate, seem to *build* and to have sufficient variety so that by the time you are done listening, you have a canvas that seems larger than each separate variation taken by itself. That's important. There are pieces called variations that are really almost separate pieces. Each variation is a kind of a separate, three-paged piece. But my *Variations* are much shorter, so that the work would be much more fragmentary if they did not build in some satisfying way. My work is meant to have more of an

architectural shape where each variation seems to be part of a fragmented whole, which, by the time you get to the end of it, is supposed to add up to a finished work.

LS: It seems to me you have established a kind of arch in this piece that becomes characteristic of so many of your works – the slow/fast/slow structure that applies to individual movements of works – sonatas – and applies perfectly to the *Fantasy*, which is in one movement. It also applies to the Piano Sonata and to the Violin Sonata, and even to *Billy the Kid* and *Appalachian Spring*. I can think of innumerable works. The classical fast/slow/fast sequence is very rare in your works. Slow/fast/slow seems to be your personal. . . .

AC: That's a brand new thought. Slow/fast/slow. Must have some deep psychological meaning. I can't think what it is right now.

LS: I have a question, Aaron, before you go on, about the

Variations. I was wondering whether, at the time of composition, you were thinking at all in terms of instrumentation.

AC: Well, since I have confessed this business of writing at the piano, obviously at the moment I arrived at these themes they were already 'instrumented', so to speak. I eventually did, many years later, orchestrate the *Variations* and they are now available also as *Orchestral Variations*. But I had no thought of orchestrating them when I was writing them.

LS: I confess that after having heard them in orchestral garb it was a lot easier for me to study the *Variations* in the original form. Prior to that I had difficulty applying myself to daily practice, partly because of the dissonant nature of the work, but, after having heard it in orchestral form, new ideas, sonorities, and touch and combinations of sound came to me as a result and transformed the piece for me completely.

AC: It would be fun to play them on the piano and then to hear the orchestral version right after it, and then to hear it played on the piano again. You could then point out more specifically how you think they connect. As for myself, I tried to forget that I had ever written them for the piano: I was trying to rethink them in terms of the orchestra.

I don't write things fast – I can't ever remember writing anything in one day. I suppose the works I wrote fastest were those I wrote in Hollywood for movies. There was a certain pressure always in getting the film out. It was costing everybody money every day that it wasn't out in the theaters. It was an investment – a large investment. But actually, it's comparatively easy to write music for movies. After all, the shape isn't so important. The shape is dictated by the scene you're looking at on the screen. That helps you decide on what form the musical accompaniment is going to take. It's not like writing in an abstract sense, such as my *Piano Variations*. But I mustn't continue on the subject of movie music. It's a different subject altogether.

The Piano Sonata I always connect with my old teacher, Rubin Goldmark. He was a very solid character. He was the first composition teacher at the Juilliard School when it was established. He was a very dignified gentleman. His uncle had been Karl Goldmark, a famous opera composer in the Germany of the 1880s and 1890s, and perhaps earlier. We got on all right. He knew the ground stuff. He knew harmony and he knew counterpoint and form. In the conventional way he could make all that clear to you, but he had no sympathy at all with the contemporary idiom. And there we parted company. After a while I stopped trying to show him any of the things that I did outside of class, though we had individual lessons. But he really should get more credit than he has been given for my early training. He was a great conservative in his time. You couldn't show him anything that was even close to Debussy harmonies without his getting sort of uncomfortable.

LS: How did you last four years with him?

AC: Well, I don't know. But it wasn't wasted time. Mr Goldmark thought of sonata form as music's highest goal. That was the thing you aimed for in the end, even more than fugue. One thinks of sonata form as a kind of dramatic form – a kind of drama is being played out – in the most typical of sonatas. It's the juxtaposition of forces that seems exciting after a fairly long time-space. A twenty-minute sonata isn't unusual. You have time to express yourself at some length, in order to add the whole thing up. In my Piano Sonata I didn't end in a great flash. On the contrary, it slows down and gradually gets less and less flashy.

LS: But perhaps more memorable for that reason.

AC: You're saying what I hoped you'd say. It isn't very different really from an honest-to-God sonata, is it? It has a first movement and a slow movement – but the last movement is rather different. It's not the usual brilliant dashing *allegro*.

LS: Were you immersed in Beethoven at the time?

AC: Mr Smit is always trying to give me forebears. No, I wasn't immersed in Beethoven. I worked hard on that piece. I'm a slow worker actually. As I say, it isn't that I work every day, but I need to get away from my work for a while in order to judge what I've done more coldly. When you're right in the thick of it, you tend to be misled, perhaps by the emotional turmoil you're in, and so you're not able to be dispassionate enough toward the thing that you've created. You need perspective. So the Sonata was written thus, over about two years.

LS: As the work was nearing completion, Aaron, weren't you

involved in travels to Latin America? The *Sonata* dates from 1939 to 1941. So was it completed in Latin America? You gave a first performance there, at any rate, so it must have been finished while you were travelling.

AC: Well, that's very good theory. I did give the first performance. Unfortunately, I can't play it any more, but I could at that time. There was a very nice composer-colleague down there named Domingo Santa Cruz.[2] He was the leader of the modern music movement in Santiago. The audiences, as I remember them, were very warm and friendly. Actually, my trip was a State Department sponsored tour, which included almost all the Latin American countries – and it left a deep impression on me. They have good composers in Latin America – comparatively unknown, who suffer, of course, from not being known. However, to come back to the Piano Sonata. It's in three movements. A first movement, the scherzo and then a finale. It's rather, oh, what would one say – it's monumental, or trying to be monumental, at any rate. It's very serious.

LS: Declamatory.

AC: Declamatory is a good word. But the scherzo is quite different. I always think of the scherzo as being rhythmically quite American. That was a big pre-occupation of mine during those years. The idea of writing a music – a serious concert music – that a European would recognize as having been written by an American. It seemed to me important, also, that we should have our own musical language, based on the great works of the past wherever they were created, but nevertheless, a music that reflected the life that we lived here and now. And since jazz had presented us with a music with a rhythmic life that no European country had, it seemed silly not to take advantage of it in our serious music. And I think the scherzo of the Piano Sonata had rhythms that I never would have thought of if I weren't familiar with jazz (I can't play jazz, but I certainly was familiar with it) – sufficiently so that it would have made a deep impression. It's a sort of dependence on the eighth note as a basic rhythmic element – different collections of eighth notes.

LS: The instructions to the pianist are very interesting: '*Mezzo*

[2] Santa Cruz (born in 1899) is a Chilean composer and teacher.

piano, delicate and restless'. It's not easy to do, even when you're nervous.

AC: The last movement is not the usual piano sonata last movement. It's rather grand and massive. As someone said – it gives off a sensation of immobility.

LS: I think that was the man who commissioned the work.

AC: Clifford Odets? No, I think you're wrong. It was Wilfrid Mellers, an English music critic and teacher who, I think, is one of the brightest musical minds alive. I know he's written about my own music in a most perceptive way. If anybody is really interested, I recommend him to you as a writer on musical subjects, especially his book called *Music in a New Found World* [*sic*]. He wrote about the last movement of my Sonata in a way that I was very pleased to read, because he seemed to say in prose what I had in my mind when I was writing it. And he even said things I really wasn't aware of consciously, but I immediately recognized them as true when I read about it. He said that the end of the last movement was a 'quintessential expression of immobility'.

The third of this trio of works, my *Piano Fantasy*, is certainly the most ambitious piano work I have ever attempted. It lasts one half-hour, without pause. I mentioned that already, but I continue to be amazed that I could write a piano piece that starts at three o'clock and ends at three-thirty, without a pause. I didn't know I was starting something that was going to continue on that long.

A fantasy is a basic musical form. It has always attracted me because of the apparent dichotomy between what is fantastic, what is a fantasy – namely, an implied looseness of form and a feeling of spontaneity – and the formal needs of writing a work that lasts half an hour. If it were all formless and gave the impression that anything might happen from moment to moment, you'd never hold the interest of your audience, or even of yourself as composer. So it does imply a formal shape of some sort. But if it's a fantasy, it mustn't be a cut-and-dried shape. It must seem to concern itself over the long spread with different kinds of musical ideas. So that my idea in writing the work, I remember, was an attempt to suggest the spontaneity of improvisation while, at the same time, keeping a discrete formal control the whole time.

LS: I would say a firm control.

AC: Firm control? Not discrete? Well, anyhow, I hope it's

controlled, but at the same time having a sense of 'Wow! – it might go any place'. It might do anything from moment to moment, which it doesn't, does it? I wrote down here what Paul Valéry published in one of his books.[3] He said: 'Two dangers never cease threatening the world. One is order; the other is disorder'. And he also said: 'The spontaneous is the fruit of a conquest'. In other words, you really conquer it, but it ends up by sounding as if it were spontaneous. Which is to say that spontaneous things aren't always the result of spontaneity. Having, in the writing, at the same time a sort of implied control – I imagine that's what he meant.

At any rate, the choice of a large one-movement form within which I worked – that definitely is a challenge to any composer. You have more room to move around in emotionally and musically, but nevertheless you find yourself enmeshed in your own thoughts and within your own musical world. When you write a single movement work that lasts half an hour without pause, you are really on your own, and you could be seriously misled if you didn't have, in the back of your mind, a controlling factor that was always there. Not every minute of the time, but at basic, essential moments – helping you to stand aside and watch what you're doing. The whole creative act, I think, is almost symbolized in the sense of not being in control, and yet, being in control. In other words, if you control yourself too much, you'll never get those bright ideas that come from letting yourself go, so to speak. So it's a beautiful balance between allowing yourself expression and yet always, in the back of your mind, somehow knowing whether it's any good or isn't it any good. I think that about covers what I was going to say about those three works.

LS: Well, whatever those fascinating aspects of the *Fantasy* from a performer's point of view are, the number and the quality of the instructions for the pianist. . . . I know of no other major work or other work for that matter that is so filled with the physical presence of the composer. It's as though he were behind your back looking over your shoulder.

AC: Sounds slightly annoying, Leo. I didn't know I was doing that. You're going to read some things I wrote in that piece?

LS: Yes, everything. And this does not take into account the innumerable '*pianos*', '*ritards*', '*crescendos*', and so on. It begins 'in a

[3] The quotation is omitted from the published score.

very bold and declamatory manner'. The next instruction is
'clangorous', then 'don't hurry'. '*Cantabile; caldo*': hot. 'Bell-like';
then 'restless and hesitant'. 'More urgent'. 'Brooding'. 'Hurry a
little' – which is not quite the same as *accelerando*.

AC: Don't you think it's quite the same thing as *poco accelerando*?

LS: You didn't say that.

AC: No, I didn't.

LS: 'Hurried and tense'. And then 'right hand as background',
which sort of upsets the normal balance between the hands. And
then comes 'agitated', 'with simple expression' and then one of
your favourite words, 'crystalline'. After that comes one of *my*
favourites: 'Delicate, "uncertain"'.

AC: 'Uncertain'? Well, 'as *if* uncertain'. I always wanted *you* to be
certain. I wanted you to be certain of uncertainties.

LS: That's the hardest thing to do. Then comes 'poetic, drifting'.
Then 'right hand freely accompanying (not too precise)', while the
'left hand controls the tempo with exactitude'. Then you've got:
'Start each trill slowly', which is not as easy as it sounds, because
some trills only last a quarter note so there's hardly any time, but
you've got to start – sort of – warmly cranking up on these trills.

AC: Sorry about that.

LS: 'Light and playful' followed by 'violent'. And 'Twice as slow,
with humour'. And then another favourite, 'Heavy staccato'. I
always think of heavy water – hydrogen bomb.

AC: But I didn't invent 'heavy staccato'. That's well known, isn't
it?

LS: I don't know of anyone who thinks 'heavy staccato'. And
you've made considerable use of 'heavy staccato' even as far back
as the *Variations*. Do you remember this one? '*Sotto voce*', and then
'muttering' – indecent story. 'With mounting excitement'. The
one that follows though is really beautiful: 'Musingly'.

AC: It suggests exactly the sort of touch that will produce a kind
of doodling effect – a toying with the note.

LS: Now 'faster and faster with mounting excitement, with always clear eighths'. 'Weighty accent on each off beat', which is very difficult because the left hand has powerful downbeats. And then 'Broader, not evenly'. That is also very difficult to do when you've spent a lifetime trying to learn how to play evenly. Just a few more. 'Slowly with atmosphere' – it creates an unusual push on the keys and comes after a big climax followed by 'full and round tone'. With the piano still quivering from the terrific and clangorous chords, I have the feeling that I must clamp a lid on the keyboard, and so I'm trying to cover all the possible areas of sound escape. And that produces what I feel is the most satisfactory equivalent of what you call 'atmosphere', and of steam escaping from under the opening of the lid. But we are not through with the list yet.

AC: Oh, we're not? I never have remembered in a public concert hall, going through, not the music, but the remarks made by the composer. This is fascinating. Go on.

LS: 'Quietly deliberate'. And then the 'left hand repeated notes are to be hurried a trifle'. That reminds me a little of *Quiet City*. Only the left hand – the lower register. And then a beautiful piece of instruction: 'floating quality', which comes at a very important point in the piece. Without those words I don't think anybody would know quite how to do it. And you write 'pushing forward considerably' until 'slowing up', trailing off to 'no tone whatever'.

AC: 'No tone whatever'? A slight exaggeration – there is some tone.

LS: I've reduced your thirty-minute piece to just about three minutes.

AC: Thank you very much. I've never heard anything like that before.

LS: My pleasure you are amused.

AC: I'm more than amused.

Appendix 2.
List of compositions by category

Stage Works

(i) Operas
The Second Hurricane (1936)
The Tender Land (1952–54)

(ii) Ballets
Grohg (1923–25)
Hear Ye! Hear Ye! (1934)
Billy the Kid (1938)
Rodeo (1942)
Appalachian Spring (1943–44)
Dance Panels (1959–63)

Orchestral Works

Cortège macabre from the ballet *Grohg* (1922–23)
Symphony for organ and orchestra (1924)
Music for the Theatre (1925)
Dance Symphony (1925)
Piano Concerto (1926)
Symphonic Ode (1928–29, revised 1955)
Short Symphony (1931–33)
Statements (1932–35)
El Salón México (1933–36)
Music for Radio (*Saga of the Prairie*) (1937)
   (later retitled *Prairie Journal* (1968))
An Outdoor Overture (1937)
Quiet City (1940)
John Henry (1940, rev. 1952)
Lincoln Portrait (1942)
Music for Movies (1942)
Fanfare for the Common Man (1942)
Danzón Cubano (1942–44)
Letter from Home (1944)
Jubilee Variation (1945)
Third Symphony (1944–46)
Clarinet Concerto (1947–48)
Preamble for a Solemn Occasion (1949)

Orchestral Variations (1957)
Down a Country Lane (1962)
Connotations (1963)
Music for a Great City (1963)
Inscape (1967)
Happy Anniversary (1969)
Ceremonial Fanfare (1969)
Inaugural Fanfare (1969)
Three Latin-American Sketches (1959–71)

Chamber Music

Rondino on the name of Gabriel Fauré for string quartet (1923)
Two Pieces for violin and piano (1926)
Lento Molto for string quartet (1928)
Movement for string quartet (1928)
Vitebsk for piano trio (1928)
Elegies for violin and viola (1932) (withdrawn)
Sextet (from *Short Symphony*) (1937)
Sonata for violin and piano (1943)
Piano Quartet (1950)
Nonet for strings (1960)
Duo for flute and piano (1971)
Two Threnodies (1971–3)

Concert Band

Emblems (1964)

Piano

Scherzo Humoristique: The Cat and the Mouse (1920)
Three Moods (*Esquisses*) (1920–21)
Passacaglia (1922)
Sentimental Melody (1926)
Piano Variations (1930)
Two Children's Pieces (1936)
    'Sunday Afternoon Music'
    'The Young Pioneers'
Piano Sonata (1941)
Danzón Cubano for two pianos (1942)
Four Piano Blues (1947, 1934, 1948, 1926)
Midsummer Nocturne (1947)
Piano Fantasy (1955–57)
Night Thoughts (1972)

In Evening Air (1972)
Midday Thoughts (1944–82)
Proclamation (1973–82)

Organ

Episode (1941)
Preamble for a Solemn Occasion (1949, transcr. 1953)

Choral Music

Four Motets (1921)
Two Choruses (1925)
   'The House on the Hill'
   'An Immorality'
What Do We Plant? (1935)
Lark (1938)
Las Agachadas (1942)
North Star (1943)
   'Younger Generations'
   'Song of the Guerrillas'
In the Beginning (1947)
Canticle of Freedom (1955)

Solo Vocal Music

Old Poem (1920)
Pastorale (1921)
As It Fell Upon a Day (1923)
Poet's Song (1927)
Vocalise (1928)
Into the Streets May First (1934)
Twelve Poems of Emily Dickinson (1950)
Old American Songs: First Set (1950)
Old American Songs: Second Set (1952)
Dirge in Woods (1954)

Incidental Music for the Stage

Miracle at Verdun (1931)
The Five Kings (1939)
Quiet City (1939)
From Sorcery to Science (1939)

Film Scores

The City (1939)
Of Mice and Men (1940)
Our Town (1940)
North Star (1943)
The Cummington Story (1945)
The Red Pony (1948)
Something Wild (1961)

Television Scores

The World of Nick Adams (1957)
Theme for CBS *Television Playhouse* (1966)

Appendix 3.
Chronological list of compositions

Juvenilia

1. *Capriccio*, for violin and piano.*
   New York, ca. 1916.

2. *Moment Musicale* (*sic*), a tone poem for piano.*
   New York, 28 May 1917.

3. *Melancholy*, for voice and piano (text, Jeffrey Farnol).*
   New York, 14 September 1917.

4. *Spurned Love*, for voice and piano (text, Thomas B. Aldrich).*
   New York, 2 November 1917.

5. *After Antwerp*, for voice and piano (text, Emile Cammaerts).*
   New York, 2 December 1917.

6. *Danse Characteristique*, for piano (four hands).*
   New York, March 1918.

7. *Waltz Caprice*, for piano.*
   New York, 1918.

8. Three Songs (lyrics, Aaron Schaffer).
   I. 'A Summer Vacation', for high voice and piano.
   New York, March 1918.
   II. 'My Heart is in the East' for high voice and piano.
   New York, March 1918.
   III. 'Night Song', for mezzo-soprano and piano.
   Marlboro; New York, July–16 December 1918.
   Manuscript with Aaron Schaffer.

9. *Sonnet I*, for piano (later included in *Three Sonnets*).
   New York, 21 September 1918.

10. *Poème*, for cello and piano.
    New York, 29 December 1918.

11. *Simone*, for voice and piano (text, Remy de Gourment).
    New York, January–16 September 1919.

12. *Lament,* for cello and piano (unfinished).
    New York, ca. 1919.

13. *Prelude* (No. 1), for violin and piano.*
    New York, August–November 1919.

14. *Sonnet II*, for piano.*
    New York, 19 April 1919.

15. *Music I Heard,* for voice and piano (text, Conrad Aitken).*
    New York, 7 April 1920.

16. *Sonnet III*, for piano.*
    New York, 13 March 1920; f.p. the composer, Salle Gaveau,
    Paris, 23 September 1921.

17. Prelude (No. 2), for violin and piano.*
    New York, February 1921.

18. *Three Moods (Esquisses)*, for piano.*
    I.   Amertume (Embittered).
         New York, 14 November 1920.
    II. Pensif (Wistful)
         New York, 8 January 1921.
    III. Jazzy.
         New York, 3 November 1921.
    F.p. the composer, Fontainebleau Concert, Salle Gaveau,
    Paris, 23 September 1921.
    Duration 5 minutes; published Boosey and Hawkes (1982).

19. *Petit Portrait,* for piano. New York, 3 November 1921.
    Duration 2 minutes; published Boosey and Hawkes (1981).

20. Sonata, for piano.*
    Class of Rubin Goldmark, New York, 1920–21.

* Except for 8, manuscripts of the above are with the composer.

Main List and Published Arrangements

1. *Scherzo Humoristique: Le Chat et la Souris* (*The Cat and The
   Mouse*), for piano.
   Brooklyn, 19 March 1920; f.p. the composer, Salle Gaveau,
   Paris, 23 September 1921.
   Duration 3½ minutes; published Durand (Boosey and
   Hawkes in U.S.)

2. *Old Poem* (originally entitled *Mélodie Chinoise*), for high voice
    and piano (text translated from the Chinese by Arthur
    Waley).
    Brooklyn, June 1920; f.p. Miss MacAllister and the
    composer, Salle Gaveau, Paris, 23 September 1921.
    Duration 2½ minutes; published Salabert.

3. *Pastorale*, for high voice and piano (text translated from
    Kafiristani by E. Powys Mathers).
    Brooklyn, 4–12 April 1921; f.p. Charles Hubbard and the
    composer, Salle des Agriculteurs, Paris, 10 January 1922.
    Duration 3 minutes; published Boosey and Hawkes.

4. *Four Motets*, for unaccompanied SATB chorus (text
    arranged from the Bible by the composer).
    I.   *Adagio ma non troppo.*
    II. *Allegro (molto ritmico).*
    III. *Molto adagio.*
    IV. *Vivo.*
    Paris, 1921; f.p. the Paris-American Gargenville Chorus,
    cond. Melville Smith, Fontainebleau School, Autumn 1924.
    Duration 8 minutes; published Boosey and Hawkes (1979).

5. Passacaglia, for piano.
    Paris, December 1921–January 1922; f.p. Daniel Ericourt at
    the Société Musicale Indépendante, Paris, January 1923.
    Duration 6 minutes; published Boosey and Hawkes (Arrow
    Press).
    Dedicated to Nadia Boulanger.

6a. *Rondino (on the Name of Gabriel Fauré)*, for string quartet.
    Paris, Spring 1923; f.p. Fontainebleau, September 1924.
    Duration 6 minutes, published Boosey and Hawkes (Arrow
    Press).

6b. Movement (*Lent–Assez Vif*), for string quartet.
    1924, rediscovered in 1983; f.p. Alexander Quartet,
    Peekskill, N.Y., April 1983.
    Duration 4 minutes; to be published by Boosey and
    Hawkes.
    Dedicated to Vivien Perlis.

7. *Grohg* (ballet).
    Paris, 1922–25.
    Duration 38 minutes; unpublished.
    Dedicated to Harold Clurman.

7a. *Cortège macabre.*
Winter 1922–23; f.p. Rochester Philharmonic Orchestra
cond. Howard Hanson, Rochester, N.Y., 1 May 1925.
Duration 9 minutes; published Boosey and Hawkes.

7b. See *Dance Symphony* (12).

8. *As It Fell Upon a Day*, for soprano, flute and clarinet (text,
Richard Barnefield).
Vienna, Summer 1923; f.p. Ada McLeish, Société Musicale
Indépéndante, Paris, 6 February, 1924.
Duration 5½ minutes; published Boosey and Hawkes.

9. Symphony for Organ and Orchestra.
Paris and New York, May–November 1924; f.p. Nadia
Boulanger, New York Symphony Orchestra, conductor
Walter Damrosch. 11 January 1925.
Duration 25 minutes; published Boosey and Hawkes (Cos
Cob Press).
Dedicated to Nadia Boulanger.

9a. First Symphony (orchestral version of 9, without organ).
F.p. Berlin Symphony Orchestra cond. Ernest Ansermet,
Berlin, December 1931.
Duration 25 minutes; published Boosey and Hawkes (Cos
Cob Press).

10. *Two Choruses*, for women's voices.
  I. 'The House on the Hill' (text, Edward Arlington
  Robinson), SSAA.
  II. 'An Immorality' (text, Ezra Pound), SSA with soprano
  solo and piano.
January 1925; f.p. the composer, Gerald Reynolds and
Women's University Glee Club, Engineering Building, New
York, 24 April 1925.
Duration 9 minutes; published E.C. Schirmer.
Dedicated to: I. Thomas Whitney Surette; II. Gerald
Reynolds.

11. *Music for the Theatre*, suite for small orchestra.
  I. Prologue.
  II. Dance.
  III. Interlude.
  IV. Burlesque.
  V. Epilogue.
New York and MacDowell Colony, Lake Placid, New York,

May–September 1925; f.p. Boston Symphony Orchestra cond. Serge Koussevitzky, Symphony Hall, Boston, 20 November 1925.
Duration 22 minutes; published Boosey and Hawkes (Cos Cob Press).
Dedicated to Serge Koussevitzky.

12. *Dance Symphony*, for orchestra (derived from 7).
New York, 1930; f.p. Philadelphia Orchestra cond. Leopold Stokowski, Academy of Music, Philadelphia, 15 April 1931 (at a benefit concert for unemployed musicians).
Duration 18 minutes; published Boosey and Hawkes (Cos Cob Press).
Dedicated to Harold Clurman.

13. *Two Pieces*, for violin and piano.
  I. Nocturne.
  II. Ukelele Serenade.
New York and Paris, January–April 1926; f.p. Samuel Dushkin and the composer at the Société Musicale Indépendante, Paris, 5 May 1926.
Duration 7 minutes; published Boosey and Hawkes (originally Schott).
Dedicated to: I. Israel Citkowitz; II. Samuel Dushkin.

14. *Sentimental Melody*, for piano.
Guethary, Basses Pyrénées, August 1926; f.p. the composer for the Ampico Recording Company, 1927.
Duration 1 minute; published in *The New Piano Book*, Volume III, Schott.

15. Concerto, for piano and orchestra.
New York and Guethary, January–November 1926; f.p. the composer, Boston Symphony Orchestra cond. Serge Koussevitzky, Symphony Hall, Boston, 28 January 1927.
Duration 18 minutes; published Boosey and Hawkes (Cos Cob Press).
Dedicated to Alma Morgenthau.

16. *Poet's Song* (originally entitled *Song*) for voice and piano (text, E.E. Cummings).
Königstein, Germany, August 1927; f.p. Ethel Luening and the composer, New School for Social Research, New York, 11 October 1935.
Duration 2 minutes; published Boosey and Hawkes (Cos Cob Press).

17.　*Lento Molto*, for string quartet.
New York, February–April 1928; f.p. (with *Rondino*) at Copland-Sessions Concerts, Edyth Totten Theatre, New York, 6 May 1928.

17a.　Version for string orchestra f.p. Boston Symphony Orchestra cond. Serge Koussevitzky, Symphony Hall, Boston, 14 December 1928.
Duration 5 minutes (with *Rondino* 11 minutes); published Boosey and Hawkes (Arrow Press).

18.　*Vocalise*, for high voice (wordless) and piano.
Santa Fé, New Mexico, June 1928; f.p. Ethel Luening and the composer, New School for Social Research, New York, 11 October 1935.
Duration 4 minutes; published Leduc/Boosey and Hawkes.

18a.　Arrangement of 18 for flute and piano by Doriot Anthony Dwyer (1972).

19.　*Vitebsk* (Study on a Jewish Theme), for piano trio.
New York and Santa Fé, 1928; f.p. Alphonse Onnou, Robert Maas and Walter Gieseking, League of Composers Concert, Town Hall, New York, 16 February 1929.
Duration 11 minutes; published Boosey and Hawkes (Cos Cob Press).
Dedicated to Roy Harris.

20.　*Symphonic Ode*, for large orchestra.
Königstein, Santa Fé, Peterborough, New York, Briarcliff Manor, New York, Juziers, France, and New York City, August 1927–September 1929; f.p. Boston Symphony Orchestra cond. Serge Koussevitzky, Symphony Hall, Boston, 19 February 1932.
Duration 20 minutes; manuscript.

21.　*Piano Variations*, for solo piano.
Bedford, Yaddo and New York City, January–October 1930; f.p. the composer, League of Composers Concert, Art Center, New York, 4 January 1931.
Duration 11 minutes; published Boosey and Hawkes (Cos Cob Press).
Dedicated to Gerald Sykes.

22.　*Miracle at Verdun*, incidental music to play by Hans Chlumberg.
New York, January-February 1931; f.p. Martin Beck

Theatre, New York, 16 March 1931.
Unpublished.

23. *Elegies*, for violin and viola.
Mexico City, Summer 1932; f.p. Charlotte and Ivor
Karman, League of Composers Concert, French Institute,
New York, 2 April 1933.
Manuscript withdrawn.

24. *Short Symphony*, for orchestra.
New York, Paris, Morocco, London, Mexico and Friend's
Lake, New York, 1932–33; f.p. Orquestra Sinfónica de
México cond. Carlos Chávez, Mexico City, 23 November
1934.
Duration 15 minutes; published Boosey and Hawkes.
Dedicated to Carlos Chávez.

24a. *Sextet* (chamber reduction of 24 for clarinet, string
quartet and piano).
New York, 1937; f.p. Arthur Christman (clarinet), Paul
Winter, Hans Rosoff (violins), Emanuel Vardi (viola),
Bernard Greenhouse (cello), and Judith Sidorsky (piano),
Town Hall, New York, 26 February 1939.
Published Boosey and Hawkes.

25. *Hear Ye! Hear Ye!*, ballet in two acts.
Lake Bemidji, Minnesota, and Chicago, July–October 1934;
f.p. Ruth Page Company cond. Rudolph Ganz, Chicago
Opera House, Chicago, 30 November 1934.
Duration 35 minutes; manuscript.

26. *Into the Streets May First*, for voice and piano (text, Alfred
Hayes).
New York, 1934.
Duration 4 minutes; published in the magazine *New Masses*,
1 May 1934.

27. *Statements*, for orchestra.
   I. Militant.   IV. Subjective.
   II. Cryptic.   V Jingo.
   III. Dogmatic.   VI. Prophetic.
Yaddo, Mexico City, Friend's Lake, Lake Bemidji,
Minnesota, Cambridge, Mass., and Peterborough, N.H.,
New York, June 1932–Summer 1935; f.p. (i) V. and VI. only,
Minneapolis Symphony Orchestra cond. Eugene Ormandy,
9 January 1936; (ii) full version, New York Philharmonic

Symphony Orchestra cond. Dimitri Mitropoulos, Carnegie Hall, New York, 7 January 1942.
Duration 18½ minutes; published Boosey and Hawkes.
Dedicated to Mary Senior Churchill.

28. *What Do We Plant?*, three-part chorus for treble voices and piano.
Peterborough, Summer 1935; f.p. Girls' Glee Club of the Henry Street Music School, New York.
Duration 2½ minutes; published Boosey and Hawkes.

29. *Two Children's Pieces*, for piano.
 I. Sunday Afternoon Music.
 II. The Young Pioneers.
Peterborough, N.H., August 1935; f.p. the composer, New York, 24 February 1936.
Duration 2½ minutes; published Carl Fischer.

29a. Arrangement of 29 for string quartet by Yvar Mikhashoff as I and II of *American Landscapes*, Set No. 1; *cf.* also 76b.
Published Boosey and Hawkes.

30. *El Salón México*, for orchestra.
New York, Peterborough, N.H., Tlaxcala, and Mexico City, 1933–36; f.p. Orquesta Sinfónica de México cond. Carlos Chávez, Mexico City, 27 August 1937.
Duration 11½ minutes; published Boosey and Hawkes.
Dedicated to Victor Kraft.

30b. Arrangement of 30 for two pianos by Leonard Bernstein.
Published Boosey and Hawkes.

30c. Arrangement of 30 for piano solo by Leonard Bernstein.
Published Boosey and Hawkes.

30d. Arrangement of 30 for wind band by Mark Hindsley (1972).
Published Boosey and Hawkes.

30e. Arrangement of 30 for clarinet, bassoon, trumpet, trombone, piano, percussion, 1 to 4 violins, and doublebass* by Yvar Mikhashoff (1983).
Published Boosey and Hawkes.
Arrangement dedicated to Lukas Foss.

31. *The Second Hurricane*, play-opera for high-school performance (libretto, Edwin Denby).

* This scoring is identical to that of Stravinsky's *The Soldier's Tale*, to which it can now form a concert companion.

New York, Tlaxcala, Mexico, January–October 1936; f.p.
The Music School of Henry Street Settlement, New York,
cond. Lehman Engel, Playhouse, New York, 21 April 1937.
Duration 60 minutes; published Boosey and Hawkes (C.C.
Birchard).

. 32. *Music for Radio (Saga of the Prairie)*, retitled *Prairie Journal*, for
orchestra.
New York and Mexico, 1937; f.p. Columbia Broadcasting
Symphony Orchestra cond. Howard Barlow in CBS
Everybody's Music series, 25 July 1937.
Duration 12½ minutes; published Boosey and Hawkes.
Dedicated to Davidson Taylor.

33. *Billy the Kid*, ballet in one act.
New York, London, Paris, Peterborough, N.H., June–
September 1938; f.p. Ballet Caravan, choreography by
Eugene Loring, Chicago, October 1938.
Duration 35 minutes; manuscript.

33a. Orchestral Suite from 32.
I.   The Open Prairie.
II. Street in a Frontier Town.
III. Card Game at Night.
IV. Gun Battle.
V.   Celebration after Billy's Capture.
VI. Billy's Demise.
VII. The Open Prairie Again.
f.p. NBC Symphony Orchestra cond. William Steinberg,
Radio City, New York, 9 November 1940.
Duration 20 minutes; published Boosey and Hawkes.

33b. Excerpts from 33 arranged for two pianos by the composer.
Duration 12 minutes; published Boosey and Hawkes.

33c. 'Waltz and Celebration' from 33, arranged for wind band by
Philip Lang.
Duration 6 minutes; published Boosey and Hawkes.

33d. Excerpts from 33 arranged for piano solo by Lukas Foss.
I.   The Open Prairie.
II. Street Scene.
III. Billy and his Sweetheart.
IV. Celebration.
Duration 8 minutes; published Boosey and Hawkes.

34.   *An Outdoor Overture*, for orchestra.
      New York, 18 October–5 November 1937; f.p. High School
      of Music and Art Orchestra cond. Alexander Richter,
      School Auditorium, New York, 10 December 1938.
      Duration 9½ minutes; published Boosey and Hawkes.
      Dedicated to the High School of Music and Art, New York.

34a. Arrangement of 34 for concert band by the composer.
      New York, 1941; f.p. The Goldman Band cond. the
      composer, June 1942.
      Duration 9½ minutes; published Boosey and Hawkes.

35.   *Lark*, for baritone and mixed chorus SATB (text, Genevieve
      Taggard).
      Peterborough, August–September 1938; f.p. Collegiate
      Chorale cond. Robert Shaw, Museum of Modern Art, New
      York, 13 April 1943.
      Duration 5 minutes; published E.C. Schirmer.
      Dedicated to Alma Wiener.

36.   *The Five Kings*, incidental music to composite by Orson
      Welles of five Shakespeare plays, for five instruments.
      F.p. Mercury Theatre, Boston, 27 February 1939.
      Manuscript.

37.   *Quiet City*, incidental music for Irwin Shaw's play, for
      clarinet, saxophone, trumpet and piano.
      New York, The Berkshires (Mass.), January–February
      1939; f.p. The Group Theatre, New York, 16 April 1939.
      Manuscript.

37a. *Quiet City*, arranged from 37 for cor anglais, trumpet and
      strings.
      F.p. Saidenberg Little Symphony Orchestra cond. Daniel
      Saidenberg, Town Hall, New York, 28 January 1941.
      Duration 9 minutes; published Boosey and Hawkes.
      Dedicated to Ralph Hawkes.

38.   *From Sorcery to Science*, incidental music for a puppet show,
      for orchestra.
      New York, February 1939; f.p. (pre-recorded) Hall of Phar-
      macy, New York World's Fair, 12 May 1939.
      Manuscript.

39.   *The City*, incidental music for a documentary film by Pare
      Lorenz, Henwar Fodakiewicz and Oscar Serling.

New York, Spring 1939; f.p. in Little Theatre of the New York World's Fair Science and Education Building, cond. Max Goberman, 26 May 1939.
Two movements ('New England Countryside' and 'Sunday Traffic') included in *Music for Movies* (48).
Manuscript.

40. *Of Mice and Men*, incidental music for the film based on John Steinbeck's novel, produced by Hal Roach for United Artists.
Hollywood, October–December 1939; New York film premiere at the Roxy Theatre, 16 February 1940. Two excerpts ('Barley Wagons' and 'Threshing Machines') included in *Music for Movies* (48).
Manuscript.

41. *John Henry*, for chamber orchestra.
New York, completed February 1940; f.p. Columbia Broadcasting Symphony Orchestra cond. Howard Barlow. Revised version (1952) f.p. National Music Camp, Interlochen, Michigan, 1953.
Duration 3½ minutes; published Boosey and Hawkes.

42. *Our Town*, incidental music for the film based on Thornton Wilder's play, produced by Sol Lesser for United Artists.
Hollywood, March–April 1940; New York film premiere, Radio City Music Hall, 13 June 1940. One excerpt ('Story of Grovers Corners') included in *Music for Movies* (48).
Manuscript.

42a. *Our Town*, for orchestra, from 42.
New York, 1940; f.p. Columbia Broadcasting Symphony Orchestra cond. Howard Barlow, 9 June 1940.
Duration 9 minutes; published Boosey and Hawkes.
Dedicated to Leonard Bernstein.

42b. *Our Town*, three piano excerpts from 42.
    I. Story of Our Town.
    II. Conversation at the Soda Fountain.
    III. The Resting-Place on the Hill.
New York, 1944.
Duration 7 minutes; published Boosey and Hawkes.

42c. Arrangement of II for string quartet by Yvar Mikhashoff as II of *American Landscapes*, Set No. 2; *cf.* also 91a and 92a.
Published by Boosey and Hawkes.

43. *Episode*, for organ.
Lenox, Mass., 20 August 1940; f.p. William Strickland, 9 March 1941.
Duration 6 minutes; published H.W. Gray (now Belwin Mills).

44. Sonata, for piano.
Woodstock, Hollywood, New York, Tanglewood and South America, 1939–1941; f.p. the composer at a concert of La Nueva Musica, Buenos Aires, 21 October 1941.
Duration 23 minutes; published Boosey and Hawkes.
Dedicated to Clifford Odets.

45. *Las Agachadas* (*The Shake-down Song*), for SATB solo group and SSAATTBB unaccompanied chorus.
New York, 25 March 1942; f.p. Schola Cantorum cond. Hugh Ross, Carnegie Hall, New York, 25 March 1942.
Duration 6 minutes; published Boosey and Hawkes.

46. *Lincoln Portrait*, for speaker and orchestra.
New York, February–16 April 1942; f.p. Cincinnati Symphony Orchestra cond. André Kostelanetz, William Adams (speaker), 14 May 1942.
Duration 14 minutes; published Boosey and Hawkes.
Dedicated to André Kostelanetz.

47. *Rodeo*, ballet in one act (choreography, Agnes de Mille).
Stockbridge Mass., May–September 1942; f.p. Agnes de Mille and Ballet Russe de Monte Carlo cond. Franz Allers, Metropolitan Opera House, New York, 16 October 1942.
Duration 22 minutes; manuscript.

47a. *Rodeo: Four Dance Episodes*.
   I. Buckaroo Holiday.
   II. Corral Nocturne.
   III. Saturday Night Waltz.
   IV. Hoe Down.
New York, Autumn and Winter 1942; f.p. (three episodes) Boston 'Pops' Orchestra cond. Arthur Fiedler, 28 May 1943; (complete) New York Philharmonic Symphony Orchestra cond. Alexander Smallens, Lewisohn Stadium, New York, 22 June 1943.
Duration 17 minutes; published Boosey and Hawkes.

48. *Music for Movies*, for small orchestra.
   I. New England Countryside (*The City*).

II.   Sunday Traffic (*The City*).
III. Barley Wagons (*Of Mice and Men*).
IV.   Story of Grovers Corners (*Our Town*).
 V.   Threshing Machines (*Of Mice and Men*).
Oakland, N.J., Autumn–19 December 1942; f.p. Saidenberg
Little Symphony Orchestra cond. Daniel Saidenberg, Town
Hall, New York, 17 February 1943.
Duration 17 minutes; published Boosey and Hawkes.
Dedicated to Darius Milhaud.

49.   *Danzón Cubano*, for two pianos (four hands).
      Oakland, N.J., 1942; f.p. composer and Leonard Bernstein,
      League of Composers Concert, Town Hall, New York, 9
      December 1942.
      Duration 6 minutes; published Boosey and Hawkes.

49a. *Danzón Cubano*, transcription for orchestra of 49.
      1945; f.p. Baltimore Symphony Orchestra cond. Reginald
      Stewart, 17 February 1946.
      Duration 6 minutes; published Boosey and Hawkes.

50.   *Fanfare for the Common Man*, for brass and percussion.
      Oakland, N.J., 1942; f.p. Cincinnati Symphony Orchestra
      cond. Eugene Goossens, 14 March 1943.
      Duration 2½ minutes; published Boosey and Hawkes.

51.   *North Star*, incidental music for film by Lillian Hellman,
      produced by Samuel Goldwyn.
      Hollywood, February–September 1943; film premiere in
      New York, Victoria and Palace Theatres, 4 November 1943.
      Manuscript.

51a. *Song of the Guerrillas*, from 51, for baritone, TTBB male
      chorus and piano (or orchestra).
      Duration 3½ minutes; published Boosey and Hawkes.

51b. *The Younger Generation*, from 51, for SAA or SATB chorus and
      piano.
      Duration 2½ minutes; published Boosey and Hawkes.

52.   Sonata, for violin and piano.
      Oakland, N.J., Hollywood and New York; f.p. Ruth Posselt
      and the composer, Times Hall, New York, 17 January 1944.
      Duration 18 minutes; published Boosey and Hawkes.
      Dedicated to the memory of Lt. Harry H. Dunham.

53.   *Appalachian Spring*, ballet in one act for thirteen instruments

(scenario and choreography, Martha Graham).
Oakland, N.J., Hollywood and New York 1943–44; f.p.
Martha Graham Company, cond Louis Horst, Library of
Congress, Washington, D.C., 30 October 1944.
Duration 34 minutes; published Boosey and Hawkes.
Dedicated to Elizabeth Sprague Coolidge.

53a.   Ballet suite from 53, for orchestra.
Bernardsville, N.J., Spring 1945; f.p. New York Phil-
harmonic Symphony Orchestra cond. Artur Rodzinski,
Carnegie Hall, New York, 4 October 1945.
Duration 26 minutes; published Boosey and Hawkes.

54.   *Letter from Home*, for orchestra.
Harvard and Tepoztlan, Mexico, Summer 1944; f.p. Philco
Radio Orchestra cond. Paul Whiteman over ABC radio, 17
October 1944.
Duration 7 minutes; published Boosey and Hawkes.

55.   *The Cummington Story*, incidental music to documentary film
for Overseas Unit of United States Office of War
Information.
New York, January 1945.
Manuscript.

56.   Third Symphony, for orchestra.
Tepoztlan, Mexico, New York, Bernardsville, N.J.,
Ridgefield, Conn., Peterborough, N.H., Stockbridge and
Richmond, Mass., July 1944–September 1946; f.p. Boston
Symphony Orchestra cond. Serge Koussevitzky, Symphony
Hall, Boston, 18 October 1946.
Duration 43½ minutes; published Boosey and Hawkes.
Dedicated to the memory of Natalie Koussevitzky.

57.   *Jubilee Variation*, on a theme by Eugene Goossens, for
orchestra.
New York, January 1945; f.p. Cincinnati Symphony
Orchestra cond. Eugene Goossens, March 1945.
Duration 3 minutes; manuscript.

58.   *In the Beginning*, for mezzo-soprano and unaccompanied
SATB chorus (text, Genesis).
Boston, February–April 1947; f.p. Collegiate Chorale cond.
Robert Shaw, Cambridge, Mass., Harvard Memorial
Church, 2 May 1947.
Duration 17 minutes; published Boosey and Hawkes.

59.   *The Red Pony*, incidental music for film based on John
      Steinbeck's story, produced by Lewis Milestone for
      Republic Pictures.
      Hollywood, February–April 1948; film premiere Mayfair
      Theatre, New York, 8 March 1949.
      Manuscript.
      Dedicated to Erik Johns.

59a. Concert suite for orchestra from 59.
        I.   Morning on the Ranch.
        II. The Gift.
        III. Dream March and Circus Music.
        IV. Walk to the Bunkhouse.
        V.   Grandfather's Story.
        VI. Happy Ending.
      Palisades, N.Y., and Richmond, Mass., April–August 1948;
      f.p. Houston Symphony Orchestra cond. Efrem Kurtz,
      Auditorium, Houston, 30 October 1948.
      Duration 21 minutes; published Boosey and Hawkes.

60.   *Four Piano Blues*, for piano solo.
        I.   Freely poetic (1947).
        II. Soft and languid (1934).
        III. Muted and sensuous (1948).
        IV. With bounce (1926).
      F.p. IV. Hugo Balzo, Montevideo, Uruguay, 7 May 1942;
      complete Leo Smit, League of Composers Concert, Carl
      Fischer Hall, New York, 13 March 1950.
      Duration 8½ minutes; published Boosey and Hawkes.
      Dedicated to: I. Leo Smit, II. Andor Foldes, III. William
      Kapell, IV. John Kirkpatrick.

61.   Concerto, for clarinet and string orchestra with harp and
      piano.
      New York, Mexico City, Richmond, Mass., South America,
      Sneden's Landing, Palisades, N.Y., Spring 1947–October
      1948; f.p. (radio) Benny Goodman, NBC Symphony
      Orchestra cond. Fritz Reiner, 6 November 1950; (concert)
      Ralph McLane, Philadelphia Orchestra cond. Eugene
      Ormandy, 23 November 1950.
      Duration 17 minutes; published Boosey and Hawkes.
      Dedicated to Benny Goodman.

62.   *The Heiress*, incidental music for Paramount film by Ruth
      and Augustus Goetz, based on the novel *Washington Square*

by Henry James, produced and directed by William Wyler. Hollywood, November–December 1948; film premiere Radio City Music Hall, New York, 6 October 1949. Manuscript.

63. *Preamble for a Solemn Occasion*, for narrator and orchestra. Sneden's Landing, Palisades, N.Y., 10 August–5 September 1949; f.p. Laurence Olivier, Boston Symphony Orchestra cond. Leonard Bernstein, Carnegie Hall, New York, 10 December 1949.
Duration 6 minutes; published Boosey and Hawkes.

63a. Arranged for organ (1953).
Published Boosey and Hawkes.

64. *Twelve Poems of Emily Dickinson*, song-cycle for mezzo-soprano and piano.
(Each song is dedicated to a fellow composer.)
I. 'Nature, the gentlest mother' (David Diamond).
II. 'There came a wind like a bugle' (Elliott Carter).
III. 'Why do they shut me out of Heaven?' (Ingolf Dahl).
IV. 'The world feels dusty' (Alexei Haieff).
V. 'Heart, we will forget him' (Marcelle de Manziarly).
VI. 'Dear March, come in' (Juan Orrego-Salas).
VII. 'Sleep is supposed to be' (Irving Fine).
VIII. 'When they come back' (Harold Shapero).
IX. 'I felt a funeral in my brain' (Camargo Guarnieri).
X. 'I've heard an organ talk sometimes' (Alberto Ginastera).
XI. 'Going to Heaven' (Lukas Foss).
XII. The Chariot ('Because I would not stop for Death') (Arthur Berger).

Sneden's Landing, N.Y., March 1949–March 1950; f.p. Alice Howland and the composer, Columbia University's Sixth Annual Festival of Contemporary American Music, McMillan Academic Theater, New York, 8 May 1950.
Eight songs (omitting III., VIII., IX. and X.) orchestrated by the composer, 1970; f.p. Gwendolyn Killebrew (soprano) Juilliard Orchestra, cond. Michael Tilson Thomas, Juilliard School of Music, New York, 14 November 1970.
Duration 28 minutes; published Boosey and Hawkes.

65. *Old American Songs*: Set No. 1, for medium voice and piano.
I. The Boatmen's Dance.

II. The Dodger.
III. Long Time Ago.
IV. Simple Gifts.
V. I Bought Me a Cat.

Sneden's Landing, September–October 1950; f.p. Peter Pears (tenor), Benjamin Britten, Aldeburgh Festival, England, 17 October 1950.

Arranged for voice and small orchestra; f.p. William Warfield (baritone), Los Angeles Philharmonic Orchestra cond. Alfred Wallenstein, 7 January 1955.

Duration 13 minutes; published Boosey and Hawkes.

65a. Arranged for SATB voices and piano by Irving Fine.

65b. Arranged for TTBB men's voices and piano (except III) by Irving Fine.

66. Quartet, for piano and strings.
Sneden's Landing, June–October 1950; f.p. New York Quartet (Mieczyslaw Horszowski (piano), Alexander Schneider (violin), Milton Katims (viola) and Hermann Busch (cello)). Coolidge Festival, Library of Congress, Washington, D.C., 29 October 1950.
Duration 23 minutes; published Boosey and Hawkes.
Dedicated to Elizabeth Sprague Coolidge.

67. *Old American Songs*: Set No. 2, for medium voice and piano.
I. The Little Horses.
II. Zion's Walls.
III. The Golden Willow Tree.
IV. At the River.
V. Ching-a-ring Chaw.
F.p. Sneden's Landing, N.Y., 1952; William Warfield (baritone), the composer, Castle Hill Concerts, Ipswich, Mass., 24 July 1953.
Arranged for voice and orchestra; f.p. Grace Bumbry (mezzo-soprano), Ojai Festival Orchestra cond. the composer, Ojai, California, 25 May 1958.
Duration 12 minutes; published Boosey and Hawkes.

68. *The Tender Land*, opera in two acts with libretto by Horace Everett.
Ossining, N.Y., 1952–54; f.p. New York City Center Opera Company cond. Thomas Schippers, 1 April 1954.
Revised version (1954–55), in three acts, f.p. Oberlin

Conservatory, Oberlin, Ohio, 20 May 1955.
Duration 100 minutes; published Boosey and Hawkes.

68a. Orchestral suite from 68.
  I. Introduction and Love Music.
  II. Party Scene.
  III. Finale: The Promise of Living.
  1957, f.p. Chicago Symphony Orchestra cond. Fritz Reiner,
  Orchestra Hall, Chicago, 10 April 1958.

69. *Dirge in Woods*, for voice and piano (text, George Meredith).
  Ossining, N.Y., June 1954; f.p. (privately) Fontainebleau
  School of Music, Summer 1954; f.p. (public) Adele Addison
  (soprano), composer (piano), Carnegie Recital Hall, New
  York City, 28 March 1955.
  Duration 3½ minutes; published Boosey and Hawkes.
  Written in honour of Nadia Boulanger's fiftieth year of
  teaching.

70. *Canticle of Freedom*, for SATB chorus and orchestra (text,
  John Barbour).
  Caracas, Venezuela, December 1954, Ossining, March 1955
  (rev. 1966); f.p. chorus and orchestra of Massachusetts
  Institute of Technology cond. Klaus Liepmann, Kresge
  Auditorium, Cambridge, Mass., 8 May 1955.
  Duration 13 minutes; published Boosey and Hawkes.

71. *Symphonic Ode*, for orchestra (revised version).
  New York, 1955; f.p. Boston Symphony Orchestra cond.
  Charles Münch, Boston, 3 February 1956.
  Duration 19 minutes; published Boosey and Hawkes.
  Dedicated to the memory of Serge and Natalie
  Koussevitzky.

72. *Piano Fantasy*, for piano solo.
  Ossining, N.Y., 1955–57; f.p. William Masselos, Juilliard
  Concert Hall, New York City, 25 October 1957.
  Duration 31 minutes; published Boosey and Hawkes.
  Dedicated to the memory of William Kapell.

73. *Orchestral Variations*, for orchestra (orchestration of 21).
  1957; f.p. Louisville Orchestra cond. Robert Whitney, 5
  March 1958, Louisville, Kentucky.
  Duration 12 minutes; published Boosey and Hawkes.

74. *The World of Nick Adams*, incidental music for television
  drama based on stories by Ernest Hemingway.

1957; f.p. on Columbia Television Network, cond. Alfredo Antonini, 10 November 1957.
Manuscript.

75. Nonet, for three violins, three violas and three cellos.
Rock Hill, N.Y., 1960; f.p. members of the National Symphony Orchestra, Washington, D.C., Dumbarton Oaks, 2 March 1961.
Duration 15 minutes; published Boosey and Hawkes.
Dedicated to Nadia Boulanger.

76. *Down a Country Lane*, for piano.
1962.
Duration 3 minutes; published by *Life Magazine*, 26 June 1962.
Commissioned by *Life Magazine*.

76a. *Down a Country Lane*, arranged for school orchestra.
1965.
Published by Boosey and Hawkes.

76b. Arrangement of 76a for string quartet by Yvar Mikhashoff as III of *American Landscapes*, Set No. 1; *cf.* also 29a.
Published Boosey and Hawkes.

77. *Dance Panels*, ballet in seven sections (choreography Heinz Rosen).
Peekskill, N.Y., 1959–62; f.p. Bavarian State Opera Ballet, Munich, cond. the composer, 3 December 1963.
Duration 26½ minutes; published Boosey and Hawkes.

78. *Connotations*, for orchestra.
1961–September 1962, Rock Hill, N.Y.; f.p. New York Philharmonic Orchestra cond. Leonard Bernstein, Philharmonic Hall, New York, 11 September 1962.
Duration 19½ minutes: published Boosey and Hawkes.
Dedicated to the members of the New York Philharmonic Orchestra and Leonard Bernstein.

79. *Something Wild*, incidental music for film based on Alex Karmel's novel, produced by Jack Garfine.
1961.
Manuscript.

80. *Music for a Great City*, for orchestra, based on music for 79.
   I. Skyline.
   II. Night Thoughts.

III. Subway Jam.
IV. Toward the Bridge.
Peekskill, N.Y., 1963–April 1964; f.p. London Symphony Orchestra cond. the composer, Royal Festival Hall, London, 26 May 1964.
Duration 24 minutes; published Boosey and Hawkes.
Dedicated to the members of the London Symphony Orchestra.

81. *Emblems*, for concert band.
Summer–November 1964; f.p. Trojan Band of the University of Southern California cond. William Schaefer, College Band Directors' National Association, National Convention, Tempe, Arizona, 18 December 1964.
Duration 10 minutes; published Boosey and Hawkes.

82. CBS *Television Playhouse* Theme.
1966.
Unpublished.

83. *Inscape*, for orchestra.
Peekskill, N.Y., April–August 1967; f.p. New York Philharmonic Orchestra cond. Leonard Bernstein, University of Michigan, Ann Arbor, 13 September 1967.
Duration 13½ minutes; published Boosey and Hawkes.

84. *Happy Anniversary*, for orchestra.
Peekskill, N.Y., 1969.
Duration 1 minute; published Boosey and Hawkes.
To mark the 70th birthday of Eugene Ormandy, and dedicated to him.

85. *Ceremonial Fanfare*, for brass ensemble.
Peekskill, N.Y., 1969.
Duration 2 minutes; published Boosey and Hawkes.
Commissioned for the New York City Metropolitan Museum centenary.

86. *Inaugural Fanfare*, for wind and percussion.
Peekskill, N.Y., 1969, revised 1975; f.p. Grand Rapids Symphony Orchestra cond. Gregory Millar, Grand Rapids, Michigan, 14 June 1969.
Duration 4 minutes; published Boosey and Hawkes.

87. Duo, for flute and piano.
Peekskill, 1971; f.p. Elaine Shaffer, Hephzibah Menuhin, Settlement Music School, Philadelphia, 3 October 1971.

Duration 13½ minutes; published Boosey and Hawkes.
Dedicated to the memory of William Kincaid.

88.   *Two Threnodies*, for flute/alto flute and string trio.
      I.   In Memoriam Igor Stravinsky.
      II. In Memoriam Beatrice Cunningham.
      Peekskill, I. 19 September 1971, II. 1973; I. f.p. students of
      Edinburgh College of Commerce dir. Neil Butterworth, 24
      February 1972; II f.p. Yoko Matsuda (violin), James
      Dunham (viola), Jeffrey Solow (cello), Sheridon Stokes
      (flute), Ojai Festival, California, 2 June 1973.
      Duration 4 minutes; published Boosey and Hawkes.

89.   *Three Latin-American Sketches*, for orchestra.
      I.   Estribillo.
      II. Paisaje Mexicano.
      III. Danza de Jalisco.
      Peekskill, 1959–1971; III. f.p. Spoleto Festival, July 1959; I.
      and II. f.p. Pan American Union Concert, Washington,
      cond. the composer, 20 April 1965. f.p. complete New York
      Philharmonic Orchestra cond. André Kostelanetz, New
      York, June 1972.
      Duration 10½ minutes; published Boosey and Hawkes.

89a. *Danza de Jalisco*, arranged for two pianos by the composer.
      1967.
      Duration 4 minutes; published Boosey and Hawkes.

90.   *Night Thoughts (Homage to Ives)*, for piano solo.
      Peekskill, 1972; commissioned for the Van Cliburn
      International Quadrennial Competition 1973.
      Duration 8 minutes; published Boosey and Hawkes.

91.   *In Evening Air*, for piano solo.
      1966, revised Peekskill 1972.
      Duration 2½ minutes; published Boosey and Hawkes.

91a. Arrangement of 91 for string quartet by Yvar Mikhashoff as
      III of *American Landscapes*, Set No. 2; *cf.* also 42b and 92a.
      Published Boosey and Hawkes.

92.   *Midsummer Nocturne*, for piano solo.
      1947.
      Duration 2 minutes; published Boosey and Hawkes.
      Dedicated to Phillip Ramey.

92a. Arrangement of 92 for string quartet by Yvar Mikhashoff as

I of *American Landscapes*, Set No. 2; *cf.* also 42b and 91a.
Published Boosey and Hawkes.

93.   *Midday Thoughts*, for piano solo.
1947, completed Peekskill 1982; f.p. Bennett Lerner, New
York, 28 February 1983.
Duration 2 minutes; published Boosey and Hawkes.
Dedicated to Bennett Lerner.

94.   *Proclamation for Piano.*
1973, completed Peekskill 1982; f.p. Bennett Lerner, New
York, 28 February 1983.
Duration 3 minutes; published Boosey and Hawkes.
Dedicated to Phillip Ramey.

94a.   *Proclamation for Orchestra.*
Orchestration of 94 by Phillip Ramey, 1985.
F.p. New York Philharmonic Orchestra cond. Zubin Mehta,
New York, 14 November 1985.
Duration 3 minutes; published Boosey and Hawkes.

Copland photographed by Malcolm Crowthers in November 1981 as he watched the sunset over the Hudson Valley from his studio at Peekskill.

Bibliography

GEORGE AMBERG, *Ballet in America*, Duell, Sloan and Pearce, New York, 1949, p. 56.

DOY BAKER, 'Aaron Copland: close up', *School Musician*, 39, Joliet, Illinois, August–September 1967, pp. 36–38.

ARTHUR BERGER, 'The Piano Variations of Aaron Copland', *Musical Mercury*, i, 1934, pp. 85–85.

——, 'Copland's Piano Sonata', *Partisan Review*, x, 1943, pp. 187–90.

——, 'Aspects of Aaron Copland's Music', *Tempo*, No. 10 (1st series), 1945, pp. 2–5.

——, 'The Music of Aaron Copland', *Musical Quarterly*, No. 31, October 1945, pp. 420–47.

——, 'The Third Symphony of Aaron Copland', *Tempo*, No. 9, 1948, pp. 20–27.

——, *Aaron Copland*, Oxford University Press, New York, 1953.

——, 'Aaron Copland's Piano Fantasy', *Juilliard Review*, v/i, 1957, p. 13.

LEONARD BERNSTEIN, 'Aaron Copland – an Intimate Sketch', *High Fidelity*, xx/11, 1970, pp. 52–55.

——, 'Leonard Bernstein on Copland and his Music', excerpted from a radio interview with Phillip Ramey, 1975; published in the sleeve notes to CBS record M33586 (*Copland Conducts Copland*).

——, 'The Absorption of Race Elements into American Music', 'Copland at 70', 'Aaron and Moses: Copland at 75', 'Copland at 79', *Findings*, Simon and Schuster, New York, pp. 74–82, 284–291, 314–16, 336–38.

ALAN BLYTH, 'Aaron Copland', *The Times*, London, 14 August 1970.

BENJAMIN BORETZ & EDWARD T. CONE (EDS.), *Perspectives on American Composers*, W.W. Norton, New York, and Princeton University, 1971, pp. 131–155.

CHARLES EDWARD BROCKHART, *Choral Music of Aaron Copland, Roy Harris and Randall Thompson*, PhD thesis, 1960, George Peabody College of Teachers, Vanderbilt University.

NEIL BUTTERWORTH, *The Symphonic Works of Aaron Copland*, MA thesis, Nottingham University, 1965.

ELLIOTT CARTER, 'Theatre and Films', *Modern Music*, xxi, 1943, p. 50.

——, 'What's New in Music', *Saturday Review*, xxviii/4, 1945, p. 13.

——, 'New Publications', *Saturday Review*, xxix/4, 1946, p. 34.

——, *Flawed Works*, Norton, New York, 1971, p. 49.

——, *The Writings of Elliott Carter*, ed. Else and Kurt Stone, Indiana University Press, Bloomington and London, 1977.

GILBERT CHASE, *America's Music*, McGraw-Hill, New York, 1955, 1966.

HAROLD CLURMAN, *The Fervent Years*, Dobson, London, 1946.

——, 'Paul Rosenfield', *Modern Music*, xxiii/4, 1946, p. 184.

——, *All People Are Famous*, Harcourt Brace Jovanovich, New York, 1974.

HUGO COLE, 'Aaron Copland', *Tempo*, No. 76, 1966, pp. 2–4; No. 77, 1966, pp. 9–12.

——, 'Popular Elements in Copland's Music', *Tempo*, No. 95, 1971, pp. 4–8.

——, 'Gift to be Simple', *The Listener*, Vol. 114, No. 2920, 1 August 1985, p. 34.

EDWARD T. CONE, 'Conversation with Aaron Copland', *Perspectives of New Music*, VI/2, 1968, pp. 57–72.

AARON COPLAND, *What to Listen for in Music*, McGraw-Hill, New York, 1939.

——, *Our New Music*, McGraw-Hill, New York, 1941; revised and enlarged as *The New Music 1900–1960*, Macdonald, London, 1968.

——, *Music and Imagination*, Oxford University Press, London and New York, 1952.

——, *Copland on Music*, André Deutsch, London/Doubleday, New York, 1961.

—— & VIVIEN PERLIS, *Copland*, Volume 1: 1900–1942, Faber and Faber, London/St Martin's Press – Marek, New York, 1984.

AINSLEE COX, 'Copland on the Podium', *Music Journal*, 29, February 1971, p. 27.

ROBERT MICHAEL DAUGHERTY, *An Analysis of Aaron Copland's 'Twelve Poems of Emily Dickinson'*, DMA thesis, Ohio State University, 1980.

PETER DICKINSON, 'Copland at 75', *The Musical Times*, cxvi, 1975, p. 967.

ARNOLD DOBRIN, *Aaron Copland, His Life and Times*, Thomas V. Crowell, New York, 1967.

PETER EVANS, 'Copland on the Serial Road: an Analysis of Connotations', *Perspectives of New Music*, ii/2, 1964, p. 141.

DAVID EWEN, *Composers since 1900*, H.W. Wilson, New York, 1969.
——, *Composers since 1900*, 1st Supplement, H.W. Wilson, New York, 1981.
——, *American Composers*, Robert Hale, London, 1982.

FREDERICK FISHER, 'Contemporary American Style', *Clavier*, No. 14, (Evanston, Illinois) April 1975, pp. 34–37.

ALLEN FORTE, *Contemporary Tone Structures*, Holt, Rinehart and Winston, New York, 1955, p. 63.

GUY FREEDMAN, 'A Copland Portrait', *Music Journal*, No. 35, January 1977, pp. 6–8.

COLE GAGNE & TRACY CARAS, *Soundpieces*, Scarecrow Press, Metuchen, New Jersey, and London, 1982, pp. 101–116.

PETER GARVIE, 'Aaron Copland', *Canadian Music Journal*, Winter 1962.

A. GOLDBERG, 'An Evening of Ballets', *Musical America*, liv/19, 1934, p. 11.

ISAAC GOLDBERG, 'Aaron Copland and his Jazz', *The American Mercury*, September 1927, pp. 63–65.

RICHARD FRANKO GOLDMAN, 'Aaron Copland', *Music Quarterly*, xlvii, 1961, pp. 1–3.

MADELEINE GOSS, *Modern Music Makers*, E.P. Dutton, New York, 1952, pp. 319–329.

MICHAEL H. HABERKORN, *A Study and Performance of the Piano Sonatas of Barber, Carter, Copland*, Ed. D. thesis, Columbia University Teachers' College, 1979.

DAVID HAMILTON, 'Aaron Copland: A Discography of the Composer's Performances', *Perspectives of New Music*, IX/I, 1970, p. 149.
——, 'The Recordings of Copland's Music', *High Fidelity*, xx/11, 1970, p. 52.
——, 'Aaron Copland: Works for Piano, 1926–48', sleeve notes, New World Records NW277.

HANS W. HEINSHEIMER, 'Aaron Copland: The Making of an American Composer', *Tomorrow*, November 1947, pp. 17–21.

ROBERT HENDERSON, '*Inscape*', *Tempo*, No. 87, 1968, p. 29.

JOHN TASKER HOWARD, *Our American Music*, Thomas Crowell, 4th edn., New York, 1965.

ROBERT JACOBSON, 'Viewpoint', *Opera News*, 40, November 1975, p. 5.
——, 'Aaron Copland', *Reverberations: Interviews with the World's Leading Musicians*, William Morrow, New York, 1977, pp. 33–45.

ROBERT JONES, 'Musician of the Month: Aaron Copland', *High Fidelity/Musical America*, 25, November 1975, *MA* pp. 6–7.

NORMAN KAY, 'Aspects of Copland's Development', *Tempo*, No. 95, 1971, p. 23.

NICHOLAS KENYON, 'The Scene Surveyed: Aaron Copland at 75', *Music and Musicians*, 24, November 1975, pp. 22–23.

JOSEPH KERMAN, *Listen*, Worth, New York, 1972, p. 334.

IRVING KOLODIN, 'Copland (and Others) on Copland', *Stereo Review*, 36, March 1976, pp. 106–7.

HERBERT KUBLY, 'America's No. 1. Composer', *Esquire*, April 1948, pp. 57, 143–5.

ALAN HOWARD LEVY, *Musical Nationalism*, Greenwood Press, Westport (Connecticut), 1983, pp. 105–127.

R.P. LOCKE, *Aaron Copland's Twelve Poems of Emily Dickinson*, Ph.D. dissertation, Harvard University, 1970.

SHARON CODY MABRY, *Monograph: Twelve Poems of Emily Dickinson*, DMA thesis, George Peabody College of Teachers, Tennessee, 1977.

JOSEPH MACHLIS, *Introduction to Contemporary Music*, 2nd edn., W.W. Norton, New York and London, 1979, p. 390.

LEONARD MARCUS, 'Some Copland Incidentals, *High Fidelity/Musical America*, 20, November 1970, p. 4.

DAVID MATTHEWS, 'Copland and Stravinsky', *Tempo*, No. 95, 1971, p. 10.

WILLIAM MAYER, 'Copland and Khachaturian', *The Musical Journal*, 27, March 1969, pp. 25–27.

WILFRID MELLERS, '*The Tender Land*', *The Musical Times*, ciii, 1962, p. 245.

——, *Music in a New Found Land*, Barrie and Rockliff, London, 1964, p. 81 ff.

——, 'The Teenager's World', *The Musical Times*, v, 1964, p. 500.

——, 'Homage to Copland', *Tempo*, No. 95, 1971, p. 2.

DARIUS MILHAUD, *Notes Without Music*, Dobson, London, 1949, pp. 253–4.

PAUL MOOR, 'Aaron Copland', *Theatre Arts*, January 1951, pp. 40–45.

GERTRUDE NORMAN & MIRIAM LUBELL SHRIFTE (eds.), *Letters of Composers*, Greenwood Press, Westport, Connecticut, 1979, pp. 293–4.

BAYAN NORTHCOTT, 'Copland in England', *Music and Musicians*, XVIII/3, 1969–1970, p. 34.

C.J. OJA, 'The Copland-Sessions Concerts and their Reception in the Contemporary Press', *Musical Quarterly*, lxv, 1979, p. 212.

JUAN ORREGO-SALAS, 'Aaron Copland: A New York Composer', *Tempo*, No. 9, 1948, pp. 8–16.

HALL OVERTON, 'Copland's Jazz Roots', *Jazz Today*, 1956, p. 40.

CHRISTOPHER PALMER, 'Aaron Copland as Film Composer', *Crescendo International*, May 1976.

VINCENT PERSICHETTI, 'Aaron Copland's Clarinet Concerto', *Musical Quarterly*, 37, 1951, pp. 260–262.

ANDREW PORTER, *Music of Three Seasons*, Farrar, Straus and Giroux, New York/Chatto and Windus, London, 1979, p. 228.

ELSA Z. POSELL, *American Composers*, Houghton Mifflin, Boston, 1963, p. 16.

PHILLIP RAMEY, 'Remembrances and Recollections of Aaron Copland on his 70th Birthday', published in the sleeve notes of *The Copland Album*, CBS MG 30071 (released in the UK on 72074, 61431 and 60139; reprinted under title, 'Copland at Home and on Tour: A Birthday Tribute', in Boosey and Hawkes *Newsletter*, Fall, 1970, Vol. IV, No. 3).

——, 'Aaron Copland', *Dictionary of Twentieth Century Music*, E.P. Dutton, New York/Thames and Hudson, London, 1974, pp. 148–50.

——, 'Copland and the Dance' (interview with Copland), *Ballet News*, November 1980, pp. 8–13, 40.

——, 'Copland at 80: A Candid Talk with the Composer about Himself, American Music and its Makers', *Ovation*, November 1980, pp. 8–14, 43.

——, Interviews with Aaron Copland published as sleeve notes on recordings of Copland's music, discussing specific works (all interviews approved and verified by the composer). On CBS: MS 7223 (72731 and 61997 in the UK), M 30649 (72872 and 61837), M 31714 (73116), M 32736 (61894), M 32737 (not issued in the UK), M 35113 (61809); on RCA: ARL1–2862 (RL 12862). (Various other sleeve notes by Phillip Ramey on CBS Copland albums contain commentary by the composer not found elsewhere: MS 7058 (72643), M 33269 (73451), MS 7375 (72809), M 33586 (61672).

CLAIRE REIS, *Composers in America*, Macmillan, New York, 1938, p. 71.

JOHN ROCKWELL, 'Copland at 75', *The New York Times* Biographical Services, November 1975, p. 1376.

PAUL ROSENFELD, 'Current Chronicle', *The Musical Quarterly*, xxv, 1939, pp. 373–376.

ERIK SALZMAN & PAUL DES MARAIS, 'Aaron Copland's Nonet: Two Views, *Perspectives of New Music*, W.W. Norton, New York, 1/1, 1962, p. 172.

WINTHROP SARGEANT, 'The Case of Aaron Copland', *Tomorrow*, June 1946, pp. 54–56.

HAROLD C. SCHONBERG, The Lives of the Great Composers, Davis-Poynter, London/W.W. Norton, New York, 1970, pp. 504–5.

ROGER SESSIONS, *Reflections on the Music Life in the United States*, Merlin Press, New York, 1956, pp. 156.

DESMOND SHAWE-TAYLOR, 'Grand Old America', *The Sunday Times*, London, 15 November 1970.

JOANN SKOWRONSKI, *Aaron Copland: A Bio-bibliography*, Greenwood Press, Westport, Conn., 1985.

NICOLAS SLONIMSKY, *Music since 1900*, Charles Scribner and Sons, New York, 1971.

LEO SMIT, 'For and About Aaron on his 75th', *Saturday Review*, 3, 29 November 1975, p. 45.
——, 'A conversation with Aaron Copland on his 80th birthday', *Contemporary Keyboard*, November 1980.

C.M. SMITH, 'Copland's "Hear Ye! Hear Ye!"', *Modern Music*, xii, 1935, p. 86.

JULIA SMITH, *Aaron Copland: His Work and Contribution to American Music*, PhD thesis, New York University, 1952; E.P. Dutton, New York, 1955.

PATRICK J. SMITH, 'N.Y. Philharmonic: Copland tribute', *High Fidelity/Musical America*, 21, February 1971, *MA* p. 26.

DORLE J. SORIA, 'Artist's Life (70th birthday)' *High Fidelity/Musical America*, 20, November 1970, *MA* pp. 4–5.

FREDERICK W. STERNFELD, 'Copland as Film Composer', *Musical Quarterly*, xxxvii, 1951, pp. 161–175.

IGOR STRAVINSKY & ROBERT CRAFT, *Dialogues and a Diary*, Faber and Faber, London, 1963, p. 47.

TONY THOMAS, *Film Score*, A.S. Barnes, South Brunswick and New York/Thomas Yoseloff, London, 1979, pp. 15–26.
——, *Music for the Movies*, A.S. Barnes, South Brunswick and New York/Tantivy Press, London, 1973, pp. 174–179.

OSCAR THOMPSON, *Great Modern Composers*, World Publishing Co., Cleveland, 1943, pp. 41–48.

VIRGIL THOMSON, 'The Cult of Jazz', *Vanity Fair*, xxiv/4, 1925, p. 54.
——, 'Aaron Copland' *Modern Music*, IX, 1932, pp. 67–73.
——, *The Musical Scene*, Alfred A. Knopf, New York, 1945 p. 125.
——, *Music Right and Left*, Holt, Rinehart and Winston, New York, 1951, p. 120.
——, *Virgil Thomson*, Alfred A. Knopf, New York, 1966.
——, *American Music since 1910*, Weidenfeld and Nicolson, London 1970, p. 49.
——, *A Virgil Thomson Reader*, Houghton Mifflin, Boston, 1981.

ARNOLD WHITTALL, *Music since the First World War*, J.M. Dent, London, 1977, pp. 91–92.

D. WHITWELL, 'The Enigma of Copland's "Emblems"', *Journal of Band Research*, VII, No. 2, 1971, p. 5, University of South Florida, Tampa.

DOUGLAS YOUNG, 'The Piano Music', *Tempo*, No. 95, 1971, p. 15.
——, 'Copland's Dickinson Songs', *Tempo*, No. 103, 1972, p. 33.

BARBARA A. ZUCK, *A History of Musical America*, UMI Research Press, New York and London, 1978.

Aaron Copland: A Complete Catalogue of his Works, Boosey and Hawkes, London & New York, 1960 (updated catalogues published in 1966, 1968 and 1973).

'Aaron Copland: His 75th Birthday', *Music Journal*, No. 29, January 1971. p. 10.

'Aaron Copland is now seventy years young', *School Musician*, 42, January 1971, p. 59.

'An Aaron Copland photo album with commentary by Mr Copland', *High Fidelity/Musical America*, 20, November 1970, pp. 56–63.

'Aaron Copland's 75th birthday', *High Fidelity/Musical America*, No 26, February 1976, *MA* pp. 224–25.

'Copland at 80', Interview with Copland by Milton A. Caine, and comments on Copland by James Goodfriend, David Hamilton, Edward Jablonski and Edith Garson, James Lyons, Phillip Ramey and William Schuman, *American Record Guide*, Vol. 44, No. 1, November 1980.

'For Aaron Copland at 80', *Perspectives of New Music*, Fall–Winter 1980, Spring–Summer 1981, Bard College, Annandale-on-Hudson, New York.

'Interview with Copland', 1st American Music Conference, Keele University, 1975.

'Composer Aaron Copland named to serve on ASCAP Board of Directors', *School Musician*, 45, December 1973, p. 53.

'Goldovsky–Copland–Schneider–Wilson make great NMC 1970 team', *School Musician*, 42, November 1970, p. 66.

'Sounds of America: a bicentennial series [Interview with·Aaron Copland]', *Music Educators' Journal*, 59, March 1973, p. 38–49.

Index

262

BEETHOVEN: THE SONATAS FOR PIANO AND VIOLIN
Max Rostal

Preface by the Amadeus Quartet
'Postscript from the Pianist's Viewpoint'
by Günter Ludwig
'Performance Problems in the Interpretation
of Classical and Romantic Music'
by Paul Rolland

This book is the first in over half a century to be devoted to a detailed analysis of the complete Beethoven Violin and Piano Sonatas. It arose from the author's wish to pass on to a younger generation more than sixty years of experience as a practising musician and teacher. Professor Max Rostal addresses himself to professional and amateur musicians alike, to students and to listeners, all of whom will derive pleasure and enlightenment from his words.

Each of the ten Sonatas is carefully discussed, the manuscripts and first and later editions meticulously compared. The musician will find technical and interpretative problems approached and solved and the music-lover a helpful listener's guide to these ever-popular masterpieces.

Professor Rostal's text is illustrated with more than 200 music examples. The frontispieces of the first edition of each of the Sonatas is reproduced, as is a portrait of the dedicatee of each work. Professor Rostal also addresses the problems facing the editor of music, and questions of dynamics, agogics, ornamentation, orthography, repeats, fingerings and bowings in these Sonatas.

Professor Rostal thus fills a long-standing gap in musical literature. As the Amadeus Quartet's Preface says of this important book, 'It is a "must" for all students and performers. It is a "must" for all lovers of Beethoven'.

'invaluable to any violinist or pianist studying these 10 sonatas'
Brio

219pp; index
Cased: ISBN 0 907689 05 1 (£12.95)
Paperback: ISBN 0 907689 06 X (£6.95)

THE MUSIC OF FRANZ SCHMIDT
Volume One: The Orchestral Music
HAROLD TRUSCOTT
With 'Personal Recollections' by
Hans Keller
And the 'Autobiographical Sketch' of
Franz Schmidt

Franz Schmidt is one of the great composers. His music covers symphonies, quartets, opera and oratorio, music for piano and organ, and his work in all of these fields reveals a master of large-scale symphonic form and one of the most substantial lyric geniuses of all time. Born in Hungary in 1874, Schmidt spent most of his life in Austria and is occasionally referred to as 'the Austrian Elgar', but despite his undeniable stature, he has not yet received the attention he deserves. Now this first of a three-volume series from Toccata Press brings to Schmidt's music the scholarship it so richly merits: Harold Truscott, an authority on Schmidt and many other composers, and himself an important composer, examines his orchestral music – the four powerful Symphonies, the *Variations on a Hussar Song* and the *Chaconne* – taking the reader and listener through each of these great masterpieces.

This first volume is introduced by the 'Personal Recollections' of Hans Keller, who knew Schmidt well in pre-World-War-II Vienna. The book also carries the first-ever translation into English of Schmidt's *Autobiographical Sketch*.

The Music of Franz Schmidt: Volume One is an early step in the rediscovery of one of the towering figures of our age. It is not so long since Bruckner and Mahler were rescued from the neglect they never deserved. Now it is Schmidt's turn.

'Schmidt's music is superbly and unarguably well made, in unhurried Brucknerian spans, and richly melodic. . . . it is . . . described in loving detail which will whet musical appetites for the unrecorded symphonies. Toccata Press does great service to the cause – and, one hopes, the real revival of interest . . .'
David Murray, *Financial Times*

192pp; index
Cased: ISBN 0 907689 11 6 (£9.95)
Paperback: ISBN 0 907689 12 4 (£5.95)